UPPER

HAND.

*To Grandpa. Thank you for taking every risk
and for showing up in the small and big ways that matter.*

Contents

Foreword

THE FUTURE OF work is already here. Global competition for labor continues to alter the employment landscape in the United States. Technology has enabled the rise of automation in manufacturing, service industries, and even white-collar professions previously considered "safe" like finance and marketing. The mass adoption of digital platforms and marketplaces like Uber, TaskRabbit, and DoorDash has fueled the rise of the gig economy and, subsequently, the gig worker. And the COVID-19 pandemic disrupted the world of work beyond anything we could have imagined, as millions of workers exited the labor force even as employers face historic talent shortages. It is not hyperbolic to say that America is in the midst of an economic transformation akin to the Industrial Revolution.

Employers and employees alike are finding themselves in unfamiliar territory. While it is tempting to focus our collective effort on returning to "business as usual," doing so would effectively leave millions of people—primarily Black and Latinx—on the sidelines. Already woefully underrepresented in STEM fields, the rapid pace of technological change has had a particularly pronounced impact on Black and Latinx workers and communities. As we stand at a crossroads, ready to chart a new path to a more equitable future, it is crucial that we bridge the gaps that separate us through a multi-faceted, multi-sector approach. We must transform the underlying systems and the mindsets that exacerbate these inequities, which are deeply embedded in the way we invest in technology and innovation, the way we educate our children, and the way we organize our cities and communities.

I first heard Sherrell Dorsey's name at an entrepreneurial conference that brought together entrepreneurs, investors, and thinkers to talk about an often overlooked but thriving world: Black tech. While the Black tech ecosystem is often covered by the media with the assumption of deficits, Sherrell's publication *The Plug* provides a more nuanced, asset-based view. Its reporting examines the challenges, the successes, and the potential of Black tech from the standpoint of people of color. Sherrell's media company is an irreplaceable source of truth for those of us dreaming of a world of work that works for everyone. Her book is a guide on how to get there.

In *Upper Hand*, Sherrell shares her experience of two decades navigating the workforce, first as an employee and now as an employer. With a personal touch and rich in anecdotes and examples, she provides insight into the tech-driven economy that has largely overlooked Black and brown communities, and also provides recommendations for how the tech ecosystem could diversify, leverage the genius of people of color, and build innovations that benefit everyone.

This book shows what organizational leaders, investors, and workers can do within the current system to make it more equitable. It speaks in an accessible voice to issues that many people of color will readily recognize from their own experience and it brings to the table an experienced, insider view of the tech world. I have drawn on Sherrell's insights many times in my own work leading initiatives to improve the education-to-employment pathways for people of color.

This indispensable book is a tremendous contribution to our collective effort to navigate the rapidly changing innovation landscape, and it serves as a guide for how industry stakeholders can work together to build a more equitable world of work.

Dr. Angela Jackson

Dr. Angela Jackson is the Managing Partner of Future of Work at New Profit, a national venture philanthropy organization that backs breakthrough social entrepreneurs who are advancing equity and opportunity in America.

Introduction

LONG BEFORE I ever sat down to write this book, the unfairness of how innovation and access are distributed among and favor certain communities over others haunted me.

After leaving my hometown of Seattle at 18, drifting across several mid-size and big cities over the years, visiting home was always deflating. First, there was the excitement of discovering an old-new city and its latest fanfare of restaurants and elevated shopping experiences, newly installed light rail systems, music venues, and galleries. But when I returned to my old neighborhoods or checked in with old friends and community folks, it was clear that they had not been benefactors of much of the city's growth.

Through the years, in my work reporting on innovation (and lack thereof) in communities of color, I have been frequently reminded of the unfairness of progress. Personally, perhaps by way of proximity, I was able to access opportunities to take part in learning the language, skills, and social networks of technology throughout my childhood and teen years.

These small, yet significant, slivers of access empowered me to position myself for a future that would be largely shaped by discoveries and advances neither myself nor my family could have imagined were on the horizon. But those same resources that empowered me were not widely accessible to the vast majority of my peers, let alone the neighborhoods and schools that we were raised in. The evidence of this loss of potential talent and potential for greater social and economic mobility is much more than a by-product of the passing of time lending itself to growing up and moving out. By design, and in the vast majority of American cities boasting deep innovation centers and entrepreneurship environments, communities of color have been left behind.

"Essential" workers, a moniker we assigned to lower-wage, service workers at the height of the COVID-19 pandemic, are largely made up of Black and Latinx people, who remain overrepresented in these fields. As technology advances and machines and robots perform many of the tasks once executed by humans, we're left with a series of questions about how we will ensure that those who are most economically vulnerable can gain access to and learn the skills of the future.

A few years ago, when I was living in Charlotte, North Carolina, I was asked to sit on a conference panel with the city's workforce development leaders and other employers to discuss the future of work in Charlotte and beyond. At the time, I was building up BLKTECHCLT, a tech hub I co-founded with my partners and friends Enovia Bedford and Freda Hendley, that provided networking and training tools to the city's rising Black tech entrepreneur community.

The panel and audience gathered in the basement of Grace A.M.E. Zion Church, a historic African Methodist Episcopal Zion church built in the early 1900s, set in the neighborhood of what is today referred to as Uptown. The conference was hosted by the Charlotte chapter of the National Association for the Advancement of Colored People (NAACP).

Unlike the many fancy tech conferences and gatherings I've attended and reported on around the country over the years, this room wasn't filled with high-profile CEOs, venture capitalists, or college graduates who'd spent years teaching machines how to think. No, these were regular folks. They were grandparents and caregivers, deacons and truck drivers. The crowd of older men and women were curious about the new world of work, some of them visibly nervous about what that new world meant for them and their families.

I'll never forget my interaction with Ms. Smith (not her real name) that day. She sat in the front row, nodding softly as the conversation ran its course, shifting between keeping her eyes locked with mine and taking notes on the piece of paper she'd retrieved from the black purse that rested in her lap. Next to her sat a slim young man who you could tell was forced to spend his Saturday morning in a place he'd rather not.

During the question-and-answer period, Ms. Smith was the first to raise her hand. She shared with us that she had lived in Charlotte her entire life and had watched the city during its many transformations, noting how she had been here before Uptown was built, when folks would have never even thought about living in a boxy apartment in the center of the city. Ms. Smith, as she revealed, was raising her grandson, the young man sitting to her right. She had been raising him since he was a toddler and she was having a hard time feeling confident that she was able to guide him into a good life and career for himself. She came to the panel because she knew technology was important but knew very little about what that meant for folks like her, trying to find opportunities for her grandson.

The city boasted a youth employment program for teens, but there were very few options for young people to get access to paid technology internships. Local schools, depending on where you attended, had few resources for computer science programs. Overall, Ms. Smith didn't have a clear guide on how to navigate the resources available in the city or whether they'd be the right kind of resources her grandson would need to get a job that paid well and would put him on the right path.

After years of toiling with ideas on how to discuss the future of work for communities of color navigating opportunities within tech, my encounter with Ms. Smith reminded me to look toward the baseline. The majority of the books on tech are written from what reads more like science fiction or are so heavily laden with inaccessible language and concepts that they offer very few solutions for the everyday person.

This book is for Ms. Smith and for those of you serving as the source of information and guidance for your families and communities.

Navigating the plethora of programs, research, statistics, and opportunities available across tech and tech-adjacent industries can be overwhelming. More important is deciding how to go about accessing these opportunities; determining the best strategies for what works requires time, knowledge, know-how, and networks. *Upper Hand* is dedicated to helping make this process and pathway easier.

Upper Hand is designed to provide and expand options to an innovation alternative—one where communities that have been historically excluded or left behind are part of the movement toward a future as technology furthers its influence and impact on society.

Upper Hand helps us think about how we strategically shape the next decade of our lives and our communities.

My hope is that you'll find and use the information in this book to your advantage, to help you think critically and strategically about how you see yourself, your family, and your community navigating the new world of work.

This is the book I'd like for you to share with your family members, friends, houses of worship, community centers, mentor groups, and more. It is not designed to sit on your coffee table. You can pick it up each quarter to be used as a frequent resource and guide as you navigate your plans for shaping your career or educational pursuits. It is filled with case studies from people who, like me, came from communities that have been historically left behind in the innovation conversation.

The resources you'll find here include definitions of terms and directories you can access and search on my website. The exercises I've pulled together are designed to spark conversations you can have with your family and community groups as you think about how to take advantage of the moment defining the future.

I can't wait to see you all on the other side.

1

Soul of a City

"Are there even any Black people in Seattle?"

I'VE BEEN ANSWERING this question over and over again through the decades, especially when I meet Black people who hail from very Black cities and are wondering exactly how Black folks have managed to build their lives, for generations, in some of the whitest places in America.

But that's truly the story of our history, is it not? Whether we had "our folks" in the room or found them missing in action, migration across land and industry—particularly within places that used to be less than welcoming—Black people have not been deterred from finding or building doors to access.

My grandfather, Jerry Dorsey III, had mastered migration and placemaking by the time Seattle's Black population began to swell in the 1960s. Born in 1933 in a colored hospital in Birmingham, Alabama, just like his sister Alberta and brother Willie, he learned early in life that the only difference between his current circumstances and opportunity was a decision to choose the path that had the potential to lead to something more.

Most Black folks left the Jim Crow South in search of better wages, better treatment in racially hostile environments, and upward economic and social mobility between the early 1900s and the 1970s. The Dorsey family was no exception. They made the transition from the bowels of the deep South, landing in Detroit, Michigan, when Grandpa was just shy of 13 years old.

My grandfather's father, "Big Poppy," found work at a tire factory in the bustling manufacturing industry that defined Detroit's local economy. "Big Mommy" worked as a domestic, like most Black women during the era, cleaning white folks' homes and doing their laundry.

Five years later, just shy of finishing high school, Grandpa was drafted into the Korean War, where he drove tanks and worked on switchboards. Like in the wars that preceded it, millions of Black men were asked to fight along with white men in a country in which they had little to no guarantee of civil rights or expected economic mobility. Grandpa could help serve his country, but he had not been granted the right to vote. Nor was he paid on par with his peers.

During the 1950s, most Black families were making on average just $1,800 annually, compared to $3,400 for white families. The stark economic racial wage gap has persisted up to this day.

By 1954, Grandpa was back living in his family's Detroit home, deciding what he would do next with his life.

One afternoon, as he sat at the family dining table, poring over applications to college and even considering an art program, there was a knock at the door. A salesman from a local trade school program would upend Grandpa's plans to "figure it out" and point him in the direction that would shape his life, and eventually my own. Grandpa only had to say yes and commit to two years of part-time training at the Detroit Radio Electronics Television School. And so he began a schedule of working during the day and attending classes at night. Around this time he'd settled down with his first wife, Anna, gotten married, and began his journey into fatherhood of two young children (my mom and uncle).

The work paid off. Just before completing his certificate at RETS, Grandpa had two job offers in hand. One was based in Jacksonville, Florida, and the other was from aircraft manufacturer Boeing. At the time, Boeing was in desperate need of workers, managing the boon of commercial and military contracts it had secured following the Korean War.

My grandfather was hired as one of many of the company's electronic technician engineers, and one of a growing group of Black workers getting access to what was considered back then a high-paying job.

Boeing expanded its employee pool of Black workers during a time America was seeing significant changes in its workforce. The company hired its first African American worker, stenographer Florise Spearman, in 1942, and by the following year had employed over 300 Black workers—86 percent of whom were women. By the time my grandfather arrived at the company nearly two decades later, in 1960, that number had surged to over 1,600 Black workers.

It was jobs like these through companies like Boeing, IBM, General Motors, and other big industry players opening their gates through need, and some through affirmative action policy in the passing of the Civil Rights Act of 1964, that helped Black people enter the middle class and chart new trajectories out of low wages and into family-stabilizing jobs in manufacturing and engineering. Very few of these jobs required any education credential beyond a high school diploma or a certificate.

Prior to the Civil Rights Act, the service sector was overwhelmingly Black and brown. Black Americans, and slowly growing Latinx populations, were likely to hold jobs in janitorial services, secretarial support staff, or in lower-level machine work that made very little room for promotions or long-term economic stability.

Boeing's move to hire Black workers in critical roles was thus monumental, particularly as large employers in Seattle like Nordstrom, Safeway, J.C. Penney, and the Bon Marché (before it was purchased by Macy's) refused to hire Black workers at the time.

The wave of corporate America's shifting attitude toward the employment of Black workers spelled change and opportunities for Black communities and became the bedrock on which my grandfather would thrive.

Ultimately, my grandfather chose Seattle for what he believed would be a calm transition. Riots were erupting across Florida as Black residents protested mistreatment and demanded the right to vote. My grandfather elected to skip out on the unrest and get to earning money to send home to his family.

So, in 1960, with his trade certificate in hand, he took off on the three-day journey to Seattle on the Greyhound bus, with one small suitcase and a few sandwiches he'd stuffed into a brown paper bag.

He arrived in Seattle a year before the iconic Space Needle was constructed, with just $30 in his pocket and no place to stay. He didn't have any "people" or family members to help him get set up. He had no housing, no vehicle, or any idea whether the job in a mystery city would work out long term. But he no longer had a choice. He'd have to make it work.

The Young Men's Christian Association (YMCA) on 23rd and East Olive Streets would be the place he'd call home for $10 a day. With limited resources, he ate only french fries, awaiting his first day of work and his first paycheck from Boeing, where he earned $2.38 an hour.

At the time of my grandfather's arrival, Seattle's Black population hovered at just over 16,000 people or just 2.4 percent of the total population, which was overwhelmingly white. A farming and manufacturing class of people ushered in a melting pot of migrants from Mexico, traveling from working in California agriculture, and Southeast Asian communities setting up businesses across the neighborhoods that bordered downtown, and a trickling influx of eastern African immigrants.

My grandfather was an early settler in a slowly changing demographic of the city. His timing was perfect, entering an industry that would have gross implications for progress as the city increasingly became an industry leader in aircraft manufacturing and then eventually software development.

Boeing proved to be the launching pad my grandfather needed to enter into a middle-class life. With a paycheck or two under his belt, he'd been able to secure long-term housing and advance within his career. He spent seven years at the company before moving on to operate the cameras at the local television station KING-TV, where he remained for 25 years until his retirement.

There's no way he could have predicted how much his life, and decision to move to a growing city sight unseen, would impact my world and an environment that would define the world's trajectory by the time I came onto the scene in 1987.

Living Legacy

By the end of 1983, my mom had finished college and left Detroit to join my grandfather in Seattle. By that time, he'd married his new wife Rosella, had my aunt Rhonda from a previous marriage, and had become stepfather to my uncle Philip.

When I came along, it was Grandpa who helped fill in the gaps. Single-parent life for my mom was facilitated by a village of family and friends. My grandfather, who lived a two-minute drive "up the hill" and had long since retired, was the designated helper of pickups and drop-offs. He was the one with the patience to help us with science products, cutting wood and metal in his garage to help me build a robotic arm for my seventh-grade science project. His knack for technology and the mundanity of retirement made me and my cousin prime targets for his evangelizing of technology into our lives.

Grandpa was also the "Inspector Gadget" of our family, known for his affinity for gizmos, the latest television and VCR home equipment, and any other electronics he could wire into his home or garage workshop. Before home security tools became the norm, a keypad would let you enter the garage. A push of the doorbell triggered a camera upstairs to confirm guests before someone would travel downstairs to unlock the door.

He even set us up with our very first personal computers in the mid-1990s, convincing my mom to get an extra phone cord for dial-up internet. As the default designated babysitter for me and my cousins when school was out, our morning activities included accompanying Grandpa to Costco for groceries and an afternoon perched in front of his upstairs computer learning how to type via the *Mavis Beacon* CD-ROM program that circulated in the computer's disk tower.

Mavis was a beloved annoyance in my grandfather's house. She was our very first engagement of a Black person's face on a software program. She looked more like an *Ebony* magazine cover model than a woman who spent her days forcing children to learn the quintessential home row on the computer keyboard. My cousin Otis and I would take turns going through each lesson while Grandpa watched a game of golf or built a new piece of furniture in his garage.

Grandpa normalized technology and our access to it in our everyday lives as a tool for learning, discovery, and a route to greater efficiency. Since he was retired and spent his days carting us around or running back and forth from the hardware store for any given random construction project he was managing at home, he had a lot of time to also curl up in front of a series of infomercials. This meant that every new CD-ROM available for the low price of $19.99 was ours to behold.

We had digital literature on the anatomy of the body with the ability to build 3D models of every body part we were curious about. Grandpa believed these tools would help us advance in our learning of science as well as technical skills. He bought us other software tools for increasing our reading comprehension, even making us sit for speed reading instruction. Grandpa was adamant about introducing tech-based learning games and software programs that were supposed to turn us into instant geniuses. We toyed around with these for a while before eventually begging to take a break from the screen to go outside to play with the other kids who would begin to gather around my grandfather's garage in the late afternoons to take advantage of the basketball hoop that hung over the garage and the miniature putting green he'd built into the yard (that to this day he has used maybe once).

What we were learning and discovering at Grandpa's was supplemented at home through my mom's intentional collection of an analog library of books and literature written by Black authors and researchers. After my dates with *Mavis Beacon*, my mom encouraged my relationship with Maya Angelou, Mona Lake Jones, Toni Morrison, Jawanza Kunjufu, Walter Dean Meyers, and other Black literary voices.

As the digital age became more accessible, and our collection of encyclopedias became obsolete, she purchased CD-ROMs like Microsoft's 1999 *Encarta Africana*—one of the early digital encyclopedias that used text, images, and storytelling to present narratives on Black Americans and African culture. For personal exposure, and for research for school projects, having access to a living, digital encyclopedia was my early experience in doing research online.

My mom was certainly no technologist, but she adapted to the environment as technology at work transformed and she prioritized its usage at home. She worked in leadership roles across social service agencies, running the office of child welfare before transitioning to nonprofit management and foster care advocacy work, where keeping up digitally was a requirement to staying competitive in the market. In addition to ensuring that we replaced at-home equipment once new models came out, Mom frequently purchased gadgets like Game Boys and Walkmans, and upgraded the home sound systems for playing Anita Baker for Saturday morning cleaning sessions. In 1996, she even owned a Palm Pilot—an early rendition of the tablets we use today.

She stressed the importance of possibility, and she did this well with how she shaped our "village." Growing up in a middle-class Black family with others who had migrated meant that our parents were keen on exposing us to "Blackness" outside of Seattle. Representing a very small percentage of the total population meant that we had all grown accustomed to being one of very few Black or brown students in a classroom. For us, underrepresentation, outside of our immediate homes and circles, was the norm.

On Saturdays, after we cleaned the house and ate breakfast, Mom transported me to the Central Area, a predominantly Black community, for a few hours of Black history and entrepreneurship learning at the Delaney Learning Center. We met at the Central Area Motivation Program (CAMP) space on Martin Luther King Jr. and Jackson Streets—a space that got its start in 1964 as a community-led initiative during the War on Poverty, as one of the first programs to receive funding from the Office of Economic Opportunity.

A group of volunteer parents and their children would spend a few Saturdays a month with us. We'd dig through history books, as they helped us contextualize the lacking information on African American experiences our classrooms were neglecting to share. We learned about the economic and cultural contributions of Black Americans. We designed projects centered around group economics and how building community wasn't just a nice thing to do, but was part of our responsibility to work together to progress and support our neighbors. We hosted car washes, where we would sell stock in our informal business to our family members in order to help us purchase supplies. We developed business plans using a curriculum designed by the national student entrepreneurship education program Junior Achievement.

I hated not being able to sleep in on Saturday mornings. Instead of letting me watch cartoons and eat cereal, Mom dragged me to class, or a board meeting, or anything that did not include me staying home and playing with my friends.

Looking back, I now appreciate the environment and understand the privilege of learning and growing in the community I did, and the intentionality our parents instilled as they shared responsibility in our growth, development, and leadership.

Delaney was just one of many groups that defined Black Seattle and my learning experience. Black legacy organizations like the Delta Sigma Theta and Alpha Kappa Alpha sororities spent time in local schools helping young Black girls explore college options. The National Society of Black Engineers (NSBE) chapters of professionals set up groups at select schools across the city to help connect students to professionals in engineering who looked like them.

Black Seattle worked hard to ensure that Black and brown kids growing up in a mostly white city had access to cultural as well as educational opportunities they might not otherwise have experienced.

Annual fundraising efforts to take students on tours of Historically Black Colleges and Universities (HBCUs) were organized by alums, and local organizations that aided in exposing students to college options helped to cover fees. Black-owned businesses like the Wellington Tea Room in Columbia City served as a staple for Black community gatherings, parties, fundraisers, nightlife, and debutante balls.

Family friends with elder children became immediate surrogate older siblings and mentors, filling me with stories about the software games and programs they were developing at their respective schools and boasting about their co-op and internship programs at companies like General Electric. They filled me with dreams of a life of success and capabilities through what I could build with my mind and my hands—just like my grandfather.

Fortunately, I would get a chance to do just that.

Just before I was set to enter high school, Mom grabbed a flyer off a community board at one of my after-school programs. A technology training program through a nonprofit called the Technology Access Foundation was accepting students for its program teaching computer literacy and programming languages, and providing college readiness and mentorship support. The program was just four years old at the time, launched in 1996, and was quietly changing the trajectory of some of Seattle's most vulnerable families. As the story went, Trish Millines Dziko retired from Microsoft as a senior software engineer and was making it her mission to help kids of color learn about and get into the field of technology.

The program would provide training, paid internship opportunities, college prep support, and a $1,000 scholarship for each year of program completion. Best of all, there was no cost to families. For a single parent who needed to keep a rambunctious teenage daughter busy and on the road to college (with added financial support, of course), my mom needed little coercion to add my name to Millines Dziko's initiative.

I was accepted and started the introduction to technology programs, taking apart and learning the different components of the computer, eventually spending time learning things like C# programming, a bit of JavaScript, ASP.NET, and my favorite class, network administration.

TAF ran the duration of the school year, with summers dedicated to paid internships with local technology companies. Twice per week, I'd hop the 48 bus from Franklin High School in Seattle's South End and get off at Judkins and 23rd in front of Parnell's corner store in the Central District—the same community in which I'd attended the Delaney Learning Center just a few short years prior. Classes ran from 3:30 to 5:30, which meant long days juggling classes and homework and taking the bus back home to the South End.

Both were predominately Black and brown neighborhoods of mixed-income economic situations and social paradoxes, harboring stories of gang violence and community picnics, Black, Hispanic, and Asian-owned businesses contrasted with street-corner weed dealers, poverty, and affluence.

Beyond the offered classes, TAF also provided SAT test prep, interview techniques, and resume building, and even took us on tours of local colleges. It was kind of like the Motown of training centers—they taught us how to walk and talk and land opportunities afforded to very few teenagers in the city. Between the fall of 1997 and spring of 2008, TAF trained 500 Seattle-area high school students of color within its technical teens internship program.

Today, the TAF Academy is a public 6th- through 12th-grade learning campus and operates as one of the leading public STEM (science, technology, engineering, and math) schools and consults with school districts around the country. Over 75 percent of the students are students of color, and many come from households where English is not their first language. Over 95 percent of students graduate on time and 100 percent of students are accepted to a two-year or four-year college.

TAF also runs a fellowship program teaching a body of diverse current and future instructors' best practices for delivering a STEM curriculum to kids of color. Two of my cousins attended and graduated from both the middle and high school programs.

Redlined to Regulation

I spent a great deal of time between the South End of Seattle and the Central District. This wasn't an accident. Most of Seattle's Black and brown communities lived between these two neighborhoods.

Seattle was no exception to the racial covenants that were established as early as the 1920s to prevent ethnic minorities from purchasing or living in homes and other property in certain neighborhoods. Before federal anti-discriminatory housing laws and the Fair Housing Act were enacted in

1968, people of color in Seattle were relegated to housing in Seattle's International Districts, the Central Area, and other neighborhoods bordering downtown. Even with laws being in place to prevent these restrictions since the 1940s, Realtors and sellers would not sell to Indigenous, Black, Asian, Italian, or Jewish Americans.

In the 1960s, Seattle was roughly 92 percent white. Over 60 percent of the Black population pushed into Seattle's Central District (the CD, as it was called colloquially). By the 1970s, that number had swelled to 73 percent Black residents.

Despite its densely populated area close to downtown, amid the suburbs, it was an undesirable location outside of the Black community. The area anchored Black home-owners and their families, as well as the Black business community.

My grandfather purchased his first home with his second wife in late 1960 in Leschi/Lake Washington, which bordered the Central Area. Today, single-family homes in that area sell for well over $1 million.

Grandpa's last and current home in the South End neighborhood of Seattle was purchased in the 1980s when the community, formerly a lot of farmland, was developing. He'd met his third wife, Rosella, and they had built their lives in a shotgun house they built on.

My mom also purchased her home in 1988 for just over $50,000. After a few years of getting acclimated to Seattle and building up her career, purchasing a property as a single woman was a major feat. Her mother had never been able to do the same. The 1940s-built home was just minutes away from my grandfather, in a neighborhood of mixed-income, multiracial neighbors with whom I grew up from the time

I was just three years old and until the time I left for college. Today, home prices in Seattle average $700,000.

My family, generationally, had moved from bouts of poverty and into the middle class through homeownership, state school education, and steady jobs that provided stability, health care benefits, and a little more access to opportunities they had not experienced growing up.

By the time I was taking the bus between school and my after-school programs, gentrification had swept a great deal of the Central District community's flavor from the sidewalk. It began with Starbucks on Jackson and 23rd; then a few of the local mom-and-pop shops were no longer able to afford the rent. It spread like a virus, until every corner was infected with the promise of boxy and architecturally unattractive apartments.

As the condos went up, we saw the demise of local cultural icons and businesses: Black-owned Liberty Bank on 24th and East Union Streets; Sammy's Best Burgers just two blocks north; Ms. Helene's Kitchen; Philly's Best Cheesesteak (now reclaimed as a weed shop); Catfish Corner; Carol's Gifts, and countless other enterprises that are now just names of the past.

Today, fewer than 18 percent of the CD's population is Black. Its white population, however, hovers over 60 percent. Do cities change and evolve? Yes. Do people and families sell their homes and move out and life moves on? Absolutely. But do all people have equitable access to the progress afforded to a select few? Not by a longshot.

Now, the community is a centerfold of high-priced condos and multimillion-dollar homes. It's a beautiful reality of progress that many of the neighborhood's Black inhabitants didn't get a chance to participate in as the city itself became a world-renowned tech hub.

Who Gets to Participate in the Future?

While Seattle battled a horrific crack epidemic in the late 1980s, as many Black communities in America had, just 20 minutes east in a wealthy suburb called Bellevue, Microsoft was stretching its legs across the workforce. After setting up shop in its soon-to-be Redmond, Washington, campus in 1986, the company quickly grew to 1,400 employees over a two-year span. There was very little mention in the Central District that the little-known software company would serve as the hub for jobs, opportunity, and economic mobility.

Today, Microsoft employs over 160,000 people across its U.S. and global offices, with 60 percent of its workforce represented in the United States. Based on its 2020 diversity and inclusion report, just under 5 percent of its workforce is Black, 6.4 percent Hispanic or Latino, and .6 percent Native American or Alaskan. The largest representation, however, is white and Asian.

For Amazon, which employs over 800,000 people across its U.S. and global offices, 7.1 percent of employees are Black (this does not include warehouse workers); LatinX workers make up 7.5 percent.

A Forgotten Workforce

A 2021 study by consulting firm McKinsey revealed that nearly half of Black workers are concentrated in occupations like healthcare, retail, customer service, and food preparation industries—essentially the jobs that provide some of the lowest-paying wages—and rarely within roles that are considered professional or managerial.

Reporting from the Brookings Institution also revealed that the highest proportions of low-wage workers are female

(54 percent of low-wage workers, compared to 48 percent of the total workforce) and women of color. Hispanic and Black workers are overrepresented in low-wage work and paid less for equivalent educational attainment. While the typical wage for U.S. workers is $42,000 per year, 43 percent of Black workers are earning less than $30,000 per year, and 52 percent of U.S.-born Hispanic workers are earning the same. Those who migrated to the United States, earn a median income of $28,000.

The Central District, like many American neighborhoods occupied by Black and brown people, was not an assumed pipeline into college, or career opportunities in general for that matter, for the descendants of those people who had been subject to redlining rules, or who had felt the impacts of terrible policy like the War on Drugs in the 1980s, which turned petty drug crimes into lifelong sentences for marijuana dealers, and enterprising opportunists whose only outlet and mentorship was from those who had been devastated by mass incarceration and a lack of jobs.

As Amazon set up shop in Bellevue and eventually transitioned to South Lake Union in 2007, just another 12-minute bus ride from the Central District, opportunity stretched again, skipping the Central District and any other local school system that had not already been a factory of talent in good neighborhoods with decent funding.

As the city built its reputation and prowess through the progress of its major technology companies, with Amazon boasting some of the largest square footage occupied by any company in the downtown community, it also increased its taste for concentrated poverty, pushing Black and brown residents out of the proximity of the more desirable area to jobs, and leaving many untrained, distant, and without the opportunity to build wealth or land the kinds of jobs that locals could have been onboarded into had opportunities for college and growth been part of the city's plan for workforce development and local investment.

Whereas my public high school had touted just a handful of Advanced Placement programs to help students earn college credit before graduation, the private schools in affluent communities where Bill Gates attended had already been well-equipped with computers and technical programs and courses that served as an on-ramp to jobs within the tech sector.

The majority of the CD's schools did not broadly offer honors or Advanced Placement courses in computer-related skills. The neighborhood schools barely offered any computer training beyond basic typing and internet navigation classes.

My middle school, which boasted a partnership with companies like AT&T for magnet status, was more an introduction to gangs and drugs than about opportunities and options for life skills that would prepare us for the jobs that existed just a bus ride away. Recruiters for the military were often at our schools, but not the tech companies.

Seattle is a proxy for most of our coastal urban cities, which have seen deep investment in their business sector with very little investment in their surrounding communities, which have been defined more for their statistics on poverty and challenges than for their workforce growth opportunities.

It is a narrative that mirrors that of every other unfortunate story about gentrification, disinvestment, and lacking economic mobility within the very communities that were left for the poor, the immigrants, and people of color who had never been invited to join in the city's progress and certainly not within a job that would govern the future. Seattle is

Oakland and San Francisco. It is New York City and Boston, Atlanta and Miami.

But how did one of the most promising cities skip over the talent pools and pipelines they claim to desperately say they value now 20 years after I left Meany Magnet Middle School in Seattle's Central District in the late 1990s?

As I recall my grandfather's story, my mom's deliberateness, and my proximity to some of the most formidable and influential technology companies in the world, I recognize how fortunate I was to have the right information at the right time to access the resources available to me.

Navigating available opportunities is not an easy task, especially when information is scattered, time is limited, or you simply don't know where to start.

I think about my grandfather saying yes to the opportunity to attend a trade program and taking the risk to leave his family behind to seek out an unknown opportunity in a land unfamiliar to him. I think about how my mother trusted that saying yes to a training opportunity for me would help me navigate a world she was uncertain about but knew that I needed to understand.

We've made getting into the technology space extremely complex. But it doesn't have to be. And although historically we've been far too often on the receiving end of exclusion, we can include ourselves in the rooms and tables that will carry us into opportunities that enable higher salaries, strategies for navigating an education that won't leave us in insurmountable debt, and career prospects that allow us to be pillars within our families and communities.

The increasing problems we face in society today, like threats to our privacy online, climate change, inaccessible banking tools, and other socially inextricable challenges, won't be solved by white guys in hoodies alone.

For too long, many of us have felt stuck without a guide. In the next few chapters, we'll take a look at the tools, researchers, entrepreneurs, language, and programs that are providing new forms of access and opportunity to what it means to be included in the future of work. The guides, exercises, and activities provided will help you with a framework for shaping your own journey in the changing and growing world of technology.

2

Rainier Beach to Redmond:
Internship Required

14 Going on CEO

My name was etched into a wood plaque, mounted on the door to my office. My badge, displaying a photo of my round baby face, strategically plaited box braids, and my full name, was fastened to the loop of my belt with authority. I'd inherited an 8×10 office space of beige walls and brown carpet that housed a black desktop computer, an ergonomically correct chair and keyboard, and a filing cabinet. At just 14 years old, I was receiving my first real paycheck from one of the most successful technology companies in the world.

It was the summer of 2002 and I had stepped into my very first internship on the Microsoft campus, feeling like a bigshot.

Never mind that it was a shared office with a college intern who probably handled much harder assignments and had more to prove. I felt like a grown-up, with real responsibilities, working with real adults, and making real money. I was no longer just the resident tech support for my family or one of several students who had gone through an extensive training period at TAF. This was the real deal. I had my name on the door of an office in a company that had defined the world of technology for the everyday person and was building what would come next.

While friends had landed camp counselor jobs or part-time retail work, I was given the privilege of learning software, marketing, and how to navigate the awkward series of conversations with adults on "what I want to be when I grow up." I attended meetings. I learned how to test and build software. I sat in the dark against the glow of computer screens with test engineers, identifying and logging bugs in programs.

Work, albeit a serious endeavor, was also a playground for me and my peer interns. We rode the company shuttles across the campus, overindulging in the bin of candy the elderly drivers put on display in the front seat. We stacked free soda cans from the surrounding refrigerators in our book bags for extra hydration for the bus rides home. We dared each other to use the company directory to email Bill Gates. We racked up Xbox games at $20 a pop at the company store and purchased software upgrades for our family computers at steep discounts. We put our $12 an hour in wages to work over our eight-week employment experience. We gathered in cafeterias for cheap or free lunches, trading stories about the top-secret programs that we were working on, attempting to one-up each other on who landed the coolest internship in the company.

For all the freedom we were afforded, and the ongoing access to every device we needed to do our job, it was the Microsoft home prototype that stamped my internship experience with the surrealness of seeing into the future. The smart home was varnished with the type of voice-activated devices we use today at least 15 years prior to the technology becoming available in the mass market. After unlocking the front door via a palm scan, you stepped into the front entrance, commanding the lights to turn on with a quick chant. The blinds followed suit, and welcoming music instantly filled the air. Before video calling was even a notion, the family room television in the Microsoft smart home was equipped with multi-sided calling for phoning friends and family. Upon setting a bag of flour or a carton of eggs on the kitchen counter, an image would display with recommended recipes. The refrigerator compiled a list of items that needed restocking once it noticed that groceries were running low. Choosing an outfit to wear for the day prompted the closet mirror to share visual recommendations based on the weather and a scan of one's schedule.

It was an integrated world where technology served as an assistant to everyday living in the context of a single-family home. It gave us a glimpse of the future we're experiencing today. The excitement of that moment cemented a world for me beyond the physical one where everything could be changed and challenged and improved through technology, and where possibility could govern how we thought about where our work might lead us next.

The smart home experience helped my imagination run wild. I brought ideas back to everyone who would listen, researching better software trends or possibilities to make operations more efficient at my respective after-school work-spaces. Those early experiences unlocked a world for me that felt accessible in the world and neighborhood I'd come from. I just had to figure out how to make it happen.

My time at Microsoft stretched into three additional summer internships. However, one particular summer, I thought it would all come crashing down. I joined a team assisting a senior lab manager who supported several engineers and IT managers in our building. I'd fallen in love with setting up and managing servers following the two semesters of my curriculum track on network management at TAF. I was overly confident, feeling like a pro at the ripe age of 16, and much too excited to handle the weight of holding Microsoft together.

Helping the lab manager was an easy enough feat until, just a few weeks into my internship experience, he informed me that he would be taking off to the mountains for a long weekend. I'd be responsible for making sure everything stayed online. Easy enough. I watched the blinking lights connected to a host of Ethernet cables and various cords lit up in the server room. On the first day of my manager's absence, I received an email from a team member that a server had gone down and they needed me to quickly help get it back up.

Without assistance and someone looking over my shoulder, I immediately froze. Trying to run through my brain and analyze all the lessons I could recall from TAF, but feeling the gaps in the information, I worked through the panic to the best of my teenage ability.

"Oh crap, I broke Microsoft," I said to myself as my palms moistened from nervous sweat. I was sure that Bill Gates himself would personally come to my office to fire me, take away my deeply discounted Xbox games, confiscate my employee badge, and ban me from the vicinity of the Microsoft campus forevermore. It would be the end of me before I could even begin.

In the midst of my melodramatic panic attack, a moment of clarity reminded me of what to do in a worst-case scenario: ask for help. I called my manager, still with heavy and hurried breaths, explained to him what happened, what I'd managed to accomplish to mitigate the issues, and let him calmly walk me through the rest. The day was saved. I kept my job, and neither my manager nor my team made me feel incompetent. Bill Gates did not have to have me physically removed from my soda-can-laden office. Thank goodness!

Those early experiences at Microsoft were lessons beyond technical skill development. They lent me environments that required self-awareness, vulnerability, perseverance, and team-building. Throughout my journey I had the privilege of working across marketing departments, building gif tutorials for internal software programs, assistant-managing a team lab, and I eventually wrapped up my last internship before heading off to college serving on the diversity, equity, and inclusion team, where I got to lead program experiences for employees, their families, and other interns.

When I made my transition to college, my managers and team took me out for a fancy lunch and gave me gift cards, cashier's checks, and a Zune (Microsoft's answer to iPods) as my summer internship came to a close.

That early experience, in addition to my training at TAF, helped me pass the "whiteboard interview" I needed to land the three-part interview process for every internship I got at Microsoft—sweaty, nervous, and wearing braids into my interview experience with three different managers, where they asked me to take apart the computer, put it back together, point out any of the software bugs, and share my thoughts on how I might go about designing a game, writing the code on the whiteboard to demonstrate my logic skills.

I was one of just a handful of interns getting access to the opportunity. While many of the students hailed from local private schools, it was a motley crew of TAF folks, and students of color, who stayed connected. Many of them went on to join Microsoft's college internship programs and land successful post-college jobs at places like Google, Netflix, Expedia, and others. A few even started and currently run their own successful technology companies.

That early internship experience gave me an advantage I didn't realize would set the trajectory for my professional life and understanding of the future of work until much later. It put me on a path toward more scholarships, like the one I received from a group of Black engineers through the Blacks at Microsoft (BAM) program. A resume with a first few years of experience at a top-tier tech company gave me a considerable boost that made landing other internship opportunities in undergrad much more seamless.

I recognize how much of a privilege it was to be born and grow up in a booming technology-centered city, and that my mom's willingness to take a chance on a training program teaching a technical curriculum she didn't understand was a tremendous move. The risk of entering the unknown opened doors for me and those of my peers, many first-generation American and first-generation college students, who also benefited from the guidance, direction, and platform these early experiences provided.

Internships continue to be onramps to social networks, job opportunities, and other connected forms of upward economic mobility. Paid training experiences at companies that set clear objectives for students and the time they spend within the company have the most impact on students. They also help to level the playing field, particularly for youth of color from less advantageous backgrounds, as summer employment can be monumental for families supported by the extra household income.

Sectors that traditionally offer paid internships, particularly in college, include business, computer science, financial services, and engineering industries. Social service industries usually do not offer paid experiences but might provide college credit arrangements.

Case Study: From Brooklyn to the Boardroom

I met Jessica Santana in New York City several years ago through a mutual friend.

Jessica grew up in East New York, which has historically been distinguished as a lower-income neighborhood in Brooklyn. Jessica was raised with her three older siblings and mom and dad in the Louis Heaton Pink House Projects. The family lived off a combined $18,000 per year for their family of six. The neighborhood may have been a far cry from any person's definition of where you might find an innovator, but the rent was cheap, hovering just under $300 per month.

The first in her family to go to college and pursue a higher education, Jessica had leveraged the Higher Education Opportunity program to attend Syracuse University in Upstate New York, where she studied accounting. The program covered much of her tuition, in addition to her room and board. She had to take out a small loan only to cover vocational activities like studying abroad in Hong Kong for a semester.

For a young Puerto Rican girl from East New York whose family never had the opportunity to dream as big as she did, she *was* the definition of the American Dream.

To keep a bit of money in her pocket during college, Jessica taught herself web design, and created a lucrative side hustle creating websites for local nonprofits in Syracuse.

An accounting internship she'd landed at Deloitte had led to an offer, but by the time she was preparing to graduate, she'd convinced Deloitte to let her work in the technology transfer office instead of on the accounting team. After about a year of helping financial services companies like banks and insurance firms keep their technology systems up to date, she transitioned to Accenture after her friend and fellow Brooklynite, Evin Robinson,

(continued)

(continued)

took a job on a similar team. This time, she would be consulting government entities.

Despite the high salary she was earning, and the resources she was able to provide back to her family in East New York, being one of the only women of color on her team wasn't exactly smooth sailing. As she and her peers traded stories about microaggressions at work, she wanted to do something about helping people who looked like her and came from the environment that she came from realize similar opportunities for their own lives.

There was no doubt that she had made it. She had landed the six-figure job and all of the benefits that came with making it out of the 'hood. She was the archetype for an urban, college-educated yuppie living it up in the big city.

Jessica followed the rules, landed the fancy and stable job, became the pride of her family, and earned the respect. And then she left.

America On Tech was born in 2014 (initially called Brooklyn On Tech, then New York On Tech) when the side hustle Jessica and Evin worked on in the evenings and weekends, training students and getting them access to tech internships, began to catch fire.

They'd launched their first event inside a free tech company event space, selling tickets and receiving donations for their cause, raising $10,000 to serve the 20 high school students they'd managed to recruit for their new program.

The press attention provided a host of grant opportunities. The inroads of support, money, and interested students became overwhelming. The following year Jessica stepped down from her six-figure salary to tend to the needs of students who were reaching out from across New York, New Jersey, and even Kansas to attend the training program that would put them on track for paid internships and, hopefully, job offers.

She did this without a plan, but with a purpose. Jessica was building a new life that ran counter to everything her family had taught her: go by the book, go to college, get married, have children, make life better for your children.

Having landed in New York from Puerto Rico a few decades prior, Jessica's family knew how to navigate survival. They weren't keen to watch her experience struggle after all her hard work to make it out of the projects and show folks in her neighborhood what was possible.

But Jessica knew that by pursuing and building America On Tech, she was designing a mission that would promise to leave no one behind.

Today, America On Tech has graduated over 4,000 students from its programs over the past eight years, through both their own training and partnerships with other student-focused organizations.

Students are recruited from public schools around the country hailing from districts where as many as 75 percent of the school population receives free or reduced

(continued)

(*continued*)

lunch and nearly 97 percent of students identify as Black or Latinx.

At AOT, students learn technology skills like web development, and are paired with top companies like NBCUniversal, Deutsche Bank, Microsoft, Postmates, and several startups, where they complete six-week internships.

Nearly 85 percent of AOT's graduating students attend a computer science or computer information program at a two-year or four-year college. Offered both in person and online, programs like America On Tech are defining new routes of access for high school students to get their shot at building the networks and necessary skills to launch their careers in tech.

Learn more about their online programs at AmericaOnTech.org.

Monica on Seward Park

Before I built my chops on Bill Gates' turf, I'd learned the world of work through Monica McAffee. "Auntie Monica," as we called her, had been my mom's nail technician since I was five years old. By the time I'd become a teenager, I'd mastered the art of styling my own hair in between visits to the salon. One day, observing my technical talent for tresses, Auntie Monica invited me onto her team to assist her with her clients in the shop a few hours a week.

I got paid in cash on the mornings before the school bell rang and twice on the weekends. Working in Auntie Monica's hair salon proved to be one of the smartest moves of my high school career. I'd take the 42 bus down the hill to Henderson Street, transfer to the number 7 for a five-minute journey down south Rainier Avenue, and walk uphill to Seward Park and Kenyon.

Auntie Monica had transitioned from a commercial shop space and into her and Uncle Kev's mother-in-law-suite-turned-hair-and-nail salon. I swept up hair from the shop's floors, restocked items, and helped to twist, braid, and converse with others to help Auntie Monica increase client turnaround and lighten her daily workload. On a regular weekend, for just a few hours, I could make up to $300— which was a great deal of money for someone who wasn't yet eligible for a driver's license. I stashed most of that cash in a certificate of deposit at the bank and spent the rest on school clothes, dances, random trips through Wendy's drive-thru with friends for the $1 Junior Bacon Cheeseburger, and gas money for friends with cars who drove me home after the school bell rang.

The shop was a learning experience in business and developing a supportive workplace culture. Auntie Monica was precise. She'd run her business for over 25 years, with clients who grew up with her. She served church folk, regular people, Black churchwomen of all backgrounds, shapes, sizes, and styles. Some were grandmothers. Moms. Wives. Sisters. Cousins. All were like family to her. She saw some of them grow up. She nurtured them and often fed them when Uncle Kev would fry chicken after a long week and serve up guests when appointments would seep into the late evening.

Auntie Monica gracefully dealt with complaints and managed feedback swiftly. She made quick adjustments as her customers offered advice on areas of improvement.

As a sole proprietor, she was the CEO and managed day-to-day operations, outsourcing financial structures to experts, cleaning and maintenance services to her mother-in-law, and brought on part-time contractors like me to help with workflow and increase her customer base without having to dedicate additional time. She filled her spare time with art, community, and performance, leading solos at her church and dancing professionally in local theater.

Auntie Monica represented fullness in entrepreneurship. She ran a business that enabled her own personal wealth journey—which consisted of a hefty real estate portfolio and a well-traveled life—on her terms.

Her brand was apparent in her discipline. Her usual wake-up time was 5 a.m., before the sun colored the sky. With a stylish outfit laid out the night before and a shop that had been deep-cleaned the night before, Auntie Monica had a natural affinity for making the place comfortable and welcoming. Her hair and nails and outfit were always pristine and stylish. She worked out and presented the best version of herself. High-end products were always on display. Her brand and her brand story riddled the community, and as a native Seattleite, the respect she earned was truly homegrown. More importantly, she was excellent at recruiting top talent.

There must have been a dozen young girls who grew up under the tutelage of Auntie Monica. Some of us were rough around the edges, had troubles in school, were unrefined, hadn't yet grown out of that awkward stage, and were still attempting to get comfortable in our own skin. Auntie Monica had a knack for both client and talent retention.

I watched her speak lovingly to her clients, advise them, and listen to their concerns. She attended their critical milestones, remembering graduations, weddings, baby showers, and even brought flowers to funerals. Even when the 2008 recession claimed the revenue of most businesses both small and large, her clientele sustained Auntie Monica's. They supported her because she supported them.

A 2021 census report on the characteristics of minority-owned businesses showed that businesses owned and operated by people of color tend to employ people within their own communities. And yet, these aren't the business owners often considered to be launching pads for educating and training the future of the workforce. Nor are they deemed to be relevant for opportunities to become accelerators of their own, or provided resources to offer paid internships.

Imagine for a second if this could be the case—that cities concerned about inclusive innovation and job growth saw these business owners as training institutions that provide psychologically and socially safe spaces for young people to learn about business and industry from people who look like them before launching into full-time careers.

Ms. Char was another woman in business who showed me early the ropes of managing and operating a small establishment. She was one of my very first dance teachers growing up. Saturday mornings, I took ballet, jazz, and tap dance classes at Rainier Dance Center, sometimes back-to-back, as a small reprieve from my mom and as part of her effort to make me comfortable with presenting and performing.

Ms. Char ran a tight ship. Parents were well-informed and provided orientation packets. We were required to be on time for every class, and be respectful if we arrived late. Student rosters, as well as accounts to manage tuition payments, were managed with the latest software.

By the time I was about 10 years old, I was assisting Ms. Char with her younger classes and was eventually asked to come on board to teach. Another weekend job was added to my roster, earning upward of $25 per hour to train younger students in tap dance basics as well as to create and choreograph.

Auntie Monica's small salon in Seward Park and Ms. Char's dance studio in the South End of Seattle were a far cry from the behemoth Microsoft campus just a few miles away. But the significance of the roles they played unlocked for me, and the others they took under their wings, a chance to see ourselves as capable of using our talents and skills to create revenue and leadership opportunities.

Where Auntie Monica had a mother-in-law suite that housed her business, and Ms. Char's dance center sat on the hill in less than 2,000 square feet, Microsoft had a dynamic transportation shuttle system shuffling busy professionals from campus to campus. Ms. Char drove us home when it got too late to catch the bus. Where Microsoft had ample access to free soda and water, Auntie Monica kept us hydrated with sun tea. Where some of my teams at Microsoft had strategy sessions, I watched Auntie Monica redesign her menu of services and work with printers for advertising her services within her community. I accompanied her to beauty sup- ply stores, where she purchased from Black-owned vendors whenever possible.

Both women exemplified their business- and customer- centric value system outside of pitch decks and investor rela- tions meetings. My experiences with these two entrepreneurs were early drivers in my professional experience before I ever stepped foot into the world's biggest software company.

Those early experiences provided me and others the con- fidence we needed to walk into larger opportunities and envi- ronments with the know-how to operate and engage with people of all backgrounds, be personable, and demonstrate accountability for the delivery of our work products.

Where Does Genius Come From?

To ignore the value of the "mom and pop" shop job experience is a missed opportunity. To discount communities shaped by inner cities, naming innovation solely to large campuses or downtown environments, misses the point that talent and skill are often cultivated in the community. And that's also from where innovation can stem.

I grew up alongside nerdy Black kids whose value was skipped over too often—the neighbors' kids, teaching themselves how to turn their home computers into beat machines, making their own music, and selling beats across marketplaces while helping their mothers pay the electric bill.

They didn't have space camps to go to or homes that were adjacent to doctors' or software engineers', but they existed and made do with what tools they had. They launched informal companies or helped the ones in their community, just like I did.

A startup isn't just what happens in a garage, dorm room, kitchen table, or tech conference. It's what builds a community, wherever that might be. And I think we wholeheartedly miss the opportunity to be transformative within our communities when we dismiss the opportunities all around us. From the coffee shop to the daycare center to plumbing services, we skip out on very necessary parts of the American economy when we hyperfocus and invest solely in things that will be high growth and high tech. Until robots can watch our children for the day, development needs to happen across the board because civics matters and ping-pong tables in the conference room aren't and perhaps shouldn't be the only reality toward upward mobility.

Never, in the history of ever, do we name the inner city or lower or disadvantaged communities as hubs for innovation, despite the creators who live there. We don't name a science building, drop 3D writing spaces into the place, or see them as anything but city problems.

Building a Tech Future in Unlikely Places

When we think about innovation, we don't often think about a city like Jackson, Mississippi, launching the next great tech company or defining the future of tech talent. And yet, this is where artificial intelligence expert Dr. Nashlie Sephus is setting up shop to define the future of innovation.

Raised in what she calls humble beginnings by her grandmother in Jackson, Nashlie studied computer engineering at Mississippi State University before going on to Georgia Tech in Atlanta to earn her master's and PhD in electrical engineering. She spent her summers interning at IBM, Delphi, and General Electric.

Her first full-time job after graduation was with a startup called PartPic, co-founded and led by entrepreneur and investor Jewel Burks Solomon, where Nashlie came on board as CTO. After about a year and a half with the company, PartPic was acquired by Amazon, where Nashlie went on to lead visual search and applied artificial intelligence research for the tech giant.

Armed with company stock and a few powerful connections, Dr. Nashlie went back home and began acquiring vacant lots to build a live/work/play/multimillion-dollar real estate development across 12 acres in downtown Jackson.

The development will take $150 million over the next five to 10 years to build and is slated to draw in festivals and restaurants, an idea to cater to the crowd and build community, with technology and innovation access on the periphery. From hosting hackathons to robotics clubs, Nashlie's plans are to make this tech district one where anyone of any profession can access the facilities, day or night, post up inside a workspace, or sit comfortably outside, in a safe space to build, create, think, and enjoy the local activities.

Jessica and Nashlie are exemplary examples of making use of their surroundings to inform their work and who they build for. They have been notably successful at navigating important spaces and bringing those resources back to the communities they come from. For both, the internship was a landing post that helped to launch them into some of the most reputable technology-leading companies.

Marking Your Own Internship Pathway

Traditional internships can take place over the summer or during the school year. But not all internships are created equal or provide enough flexibility for students who may be nontraditional students and need more options for being able to learn skills and build up a portfolio.

Opportunities to get started and break into tech and other careers are expanding, especially with jobs and internships moving online, or externships being offered through vocational schools and boot camps.

Case Study: The Sprinternship

Women and students of color are often at a disadvantage when it comes to taking on internships, hindering their opportunities to build relationships and connections in the technology sector.

To help close the gap, Break Through Tech launched a new idea called a "Sprinternship," which gives women and other underrepresented students a shot at interning at tech companies over the course of a traditional break during the academic year.

Piloted at the City University of New York, Cornell Tech, and other schools since 2018, the program provides paid internships to computer science students over the three-week winter break between the fall and spring semesters. Students build connections with potential employers and develop portfolios of their work experience to be used as they complete their computer science degrees and enter the workforce.

The program has since expanded to Chicago and Washington, DC.

Over 80 companies have hosted over 700 student internships since the program's inception. Students are making connections and getting access to networks they might not have otherwise had it not been for the existence of the program.

Action Items

- Find out which businesses in your city offer internship or apprenticeship opportunities for students within your area—start with your own community.

- Create your own internship program if there isn't one by pitching to a company in your community. Detail the skills you have that they need and what you can do to help them improve their business. Ask for a two-week trial or project to help them see why they should bring you onto their team.

- Tap your local workforce development program to see what training programs they offer that also place you in an apprenticeship with a company.

- Find online internship programs that allow you to work from home—keep a plan of what you want to learn and build relationships with your colleagues for future job recommendations.

- Seek fellowship opportunities that are shorter in time and allow for travel or learning plus a stipend to help you transition in your skill (profellow.org is an excellent research tool that lets you search for opportunities here and abroad).

- Build your network by joining associations and groups that are connected to opportunities within technology—be it a local boot camp or meetup group—and ask around about fellowship opportunities.

3

Playing the Game Around Us

The True Cost of College

$125,000 in principal amortized over the past 10 years with an average 6 percent interest rate is what I have paid for the privilege of telling the world that I followed the formula of going to college. And this is with the scholarships and grants I managed to hustle to help pay for both my undergraduate and graduate education.

Like many of the millions of millennials entering a dismal job market that had been severely impacted by the 2008 recession, I'd felt bamboozled right out of undergrad. The formula that had been preached to us over the last 20 years did not account for an economic fallout, low salaries, and job prospects that made the four-year commitment of time and money feel like a waste. There was no golden ticket at the end of our time served.

No one cared that I had a degree when the sky was falling.

It was mostly hustling and the wake of an increasingly digital environment that helped me to stand out in the job market. In fact, most of the internships and eventually post-graduate jobs and freelance work I managed to land were the result of having created a dynamic public persona and reputation online.

As blogging became popular in the early 2000s, I joined the bandwagon, crafting sentences and manipulating WordPress templates. I carved out a niche in a very crowded, yet lucrative, culture of the emerging and early "influencers" covering beauty, fashion, and other general interest sites covering cultural trends.

A student of the Fashion Institute of Technology, determined to land gigs within the industry with startups and social-mission-driven brands, I turned the insights I was learning within my corporate social responsibility courses and lectures I attended at local universities, along with the conferences I hacked my way into via volunteering to run social media coverage, into material for my blog. I mostly covered environmental stewardship within the fashion industry, with a focus on chemical-free and nontoxic beauty products. The category had seen tremendous growth by 2007 and I applied my learnings to trends in product usage for Black and brown women, who were noticeably being ignored in the sector's growth, as options for chemical-free makeup and products weren't directly marketed to this demographic. I inserted my learnings and cited research from the policy conferences I attended on chemicals in cosmetics and their disproportionate and disruptive impact on communities of color. At the time, scientists had been studying how cosmetics, and specific products used by Black and Latinx communities, had been increasing hormone disruption, accounting for greater estrogen exposure that was leading to young children beginning puberty as early as six years old!

My blog, Organic Beauty Vixen, covered both the glam available for those looking to switch from chemical-laden products (with frequent mentions of the work being done in the industry, thanks to platforms and databases like the Environmental Working Group) as well as what I was learning in my research. I was helping my audience understand that products picked up at the beauty supply and 99-cent store were some of the most unregulated products on the market.

An internship with a startup cosmetics company introduced me to the perils of chemicals in cosmetics on compromised skin. I learned the industry through attending and working on tradeshow events and learning about changes coming to the industry. Through my obsession with understanding everything there was about the industry and the social justice issues plaguing it, I developed my communication skills, and demonstrated through my blog an ability to brand, synthesize, and build an audience.

Carving a voice and a brand for myself in an otherwise tough employment market was an unknowing hack that helped me survive. Advertising networks onboarded me to their clients. I earned a few thousand dollars each month for ad placements from media networks that took full advantage of the more than 20,000 monthly visitors I was able to bring to my website. I received a ton of products I shared with friends and pushed off as gifts. Invites to brand parties and launches at penthouses in chic hotels were the norm. The money I earned, accumulated over a few years of consistent blogging, helped to cover my rent and keep me afloat as I managed classes, an internship, a part-time business, and sometimes evening retail shifts.

Having a digital presence, a few internships in the fashion industry, and a few portfolio projects under my belt were what helped to set me apart. More important: my blog helped me create a living and breathing resume that caught the attention of my first employer out of college.

My first employer, a famous couture fashion designer who valued the use of sustainable materials in her designs, reached out to me after having come across my blog. After a quick phone interview, she asked me to join the marketing team tasked with rebuilding her line of beauty and wellness products she would be relaunching that summer.

That same designer had attended the very same institution I would be graduating from just a week following our phone interview. She also happened to be the keynote speaker at the graduation. I graduated on a Friday at Radio City Music

Hall in the heart of Times Square and embarked on my first day of work that following Monday at 10 a.m. sharp at the company's store near Columbus Circle.

While I was fortunate to land a job right out of college, the market was still grim. Every business took a hit, and as fast fashion became a staple in most people's wardrobes and retail buyers began cutting back on their orders as people held on to what money they could, not even six months later, I found myself back to the hustle. I freelanced where I could, trying to squeeze everything out of my blog revenue and interviewing for jobs that were often receiving hundreds of applicants for just one open spot at a company.

The designer's business took a tremendous hit and I saw it coming when after about a week on the job, she let go of a handful of people. Each week, I'd come to work and another colleague's email would be deactivated.

Morale took a hit as well. The designer, who also held the reins as CEO, sent a company-wide email attempting to explain the present conditions. She told us that with the economic climate, there were many people who were forced out of the job market and that the chances were that many of them wouldn't find work again for a very long time. The world, and quite certainly the industry we were in, was changing drastically. A big-time retailer had discontinued the development of the brand's accessible line, and overall retail sales for high-end apparel had slowed. We were all fighting for our lives.

Folks my mother's age, who had been laid off from their long-time corporate careers, were turning to retail management and any other work they could get to put food on the table.

Keeping the Harlem apartment I had proudly moved into alone and without roommates following my first post-college job was no longer sustainable.

Between my cousin coming to town for an internship to share in the rent, and friends here and there borrowing the sofa, we scraped by with pure adrenaline, Trader Joe's pasta and vodka sauce, and three-buck-chuck wine, determined to live our New York City dreams and land on our feet.

But there was no navigating a world we hadn't been prepared for. The promise of a college education being the ticket to economic stability and an "adult" life quickly faded under the ashes of missed student loan payments and an extremely high cost of living.

It was an extremely humbling and also unfair reality. And no relief for students who had played the game would be on the way. Just seven months into my two-year lease, I could no longer keep up with my New York City dream. So I packed up my Harlem apartment and moved back home to Seattle, hoping my past relationships and my New York City energy would land me someplace reputable. I was looking for a place to land because at 22 years old, with a degree in hand, I felt like I had failed. Instead of "making it" in New York City, I'd burned out. I was broke and embarrassed.

I went from complete independence to depending on family and friends. My mom and best friend would even spot me a few dollars as I waited for delayed freelance checks in the mail. I grew weary of the onslaught of interviews where I went from being a top candidate for corporate jobs in marketing and social media to getting beat out by someone with much more experience who had been willing to take a pay cut.

Nothing seemed to work. I went back to helping Auntie Monica in the salon. I went back to my old dance studios and taught adult classes. I had no car, no permanent housing, and wasn't in a relationship. I'd laugh with friends over cocktails they'd cover for me about how it felt like my rock bottom, and nothing could get any worse.

I lived with family friends and sometimes my mom, who would spot me a few dollars as I arranged informational interviews over coffee with professionals in local retail industries I was looking to network my way into.

The following years would prove to be an exercise in tenacity and resilience. I had resources from friends and family to help me sustain the blow, but ultimately I was outhustled by a prescribed value system that purported to value the high cost of an education that provided me with very little return.

Death to the Debt

According to the U.S. Department of Education, student loan borrowers owe a collective $1.6 trillion between private and federal student loan debt. The impact of this debt has led to a life of delay: of homeownership, marriages, birthrates, and overall wealth accumulation across our generation.

Based on education loan debt data, more than 35 million borrowers owe more than $36,000. Black and African American college graduates owe an average of $25,000 more in student loan debt than white college graduates. Other factors at play include what majors students choose in their undergraduate experiences that also limit their overall earning power.

Largely, students of color are most likely to avoid expensive majors in areas like engineering and the sciences. Research by the Center for American Progress, conducted in 2018, revealed that Black students over-index in the social and health sciences compared to their white counterparts, but growth over the years in the selection of computer sciences was also on par with overall bachelor's degrees earned between 2013 and 2015.

My college career hadn't been marked by a real decision on what would be the future of the economy. It was hyper-focused on creative play and exploration and discovery—a totally fine pursuit had I had something aligned with the current or future market that could easily be transferable to a technical industry where my skills would be in demand.

Considering my time at TAF, and the influences of computer scientists within my orbit, I elected not to study computer science. I wasn't thrilled with the idea of sitting in a room coding all day. I needed greater stimulation, human interaction, and movement in a career; I just hadn't figured out what that would be yet. So I remained a generalist as a marketing and business major, finding marginal success working for startup beauty and fashion companies, launching campaigns and mildly assisting with e-commerce initiatives and the burgeoning specialty of social media marketing.

Had I been able to walk away with deeper technical skills, landing a more stable opportunity, the financial trajectory of my experience could have changed.

A New Kind of Education Future

At the same time that I was wrapping up my college education, micro-credentialing and online courses through platforms such as Skillshare, edX, Udemy, and others began to populate the internet. Companies were looking for people who could come in and on day one, get the work done.

From learning the basics of data analysis to introductions to computer science to project management or statistical analysis, these programs offered a self-guided or live curriculum and training that was starting to change the way we learned and who we learned from. Elite institutions like Harvard and Yale began sharing course instruction. And while these courses weren't always completed by participants, such programs marked a changing landscape of accessible education not compounded or confined to an admissions exam or application.

Learning was becoming democratized and somewhat more accessible in the early 2010s.

These days, the dependency on obtaining a four-year degree from a prestigious university is almost becoming antiquated. In my days at Microsoft, very few of my bosses had college degrees. Many were self-taught through coding books, hacker groups, or internal training programs.

Today, access to online education is slowly slimming the divide between knowledge accessibility and knowledge acquired. This looks like the explosion of massive online open courses (MOOCs), where anyone on the internet could access elite university curriculum and professors. Though the course completion rate is between 5 and 15 percent, the availability of these tools provided a portal through which people could learn what they wanted when they wanted.

Companies like IBM, Amazon, CompTIA, Google, and others were providing certificates and credentialing on their own platforms for low or no cost to students. These programs still exist today and provide direct training on their platforms, getting to the core of industry best practices, and providing some form of a certificate of completion or credentialing that documents a skill.

Online education and the availability of coding and technical programs have also picked up steam, as isolated skills training enables the opportunity for quick skill-building outside of long-form university environments.

Let's put this into perspective. The cost of a four-year college education has doubled for state universities and has more than tripled for private universities. This is not a direct reflection of improvement of education, however, but of a higher spend on more administrative expenses, making the return on investment, depending on major pursued, a questionable endeavor.

Estimates show that as the growth rate of tuition increases, the cost of a college education could reach upwards of $130,000 per year by 2030. This, of course, does not account for any financial aid offered by schools but represents the tremendous investment needed to earn this long-standing credential that has, in the past several decades, defined the earning potential for most Americans.

The research that we've been told about ad nauseum is that earning a bachelor's degree means almost $1 million more earned over the course of a lifetime compared to someone with just a high school diploma. And the numbers potentially increase the more education earned.

Options for those hoping to skip the four-year financial commitment, or who do not have the option to attend, are expanding. Enter boot camps, certificate programs, and other forms of training.

The cost differential is astounding. Tuition averages for tech-specific boot camp or certificate programs can range from just a few thousand dollars to upwards of $20,000, with the median cost at $13,000. The industry itself is cozying up to big tech firms that are putting respect on their names.

The road from boot camp to career is narrowing. Companies like SpaceX, Google, Apple, Starbucks, Nordstrom, and others have said they're no longer requiring a four-year degree for some of their jobs. These employers are recognizing that hard work, grit, and perseverance aren't restricted to those who were able to graduate from a four-year college program.

And considering that attending college is often a privilege for those who can afford it or have the opportunity, industries across the board are considering how certifications and other forms of credentialing should be considered when recruiting and hiring more diverse candidates.

For many, these options present a great deal of opportunity to get a foot in the door and continue to learn, reskill, or level up for greater salaries and opportunities.

From programs like Flatiron School to General Assembly, boot camp programs have trained an estimated more than 39,000 students in 2019 alone. Boot camps across 600-plus schools tout a 90 percent or more placement rate in jobs and careers with top-tier companies. Prospects are opening what once was only available to those hailing from prestigious universities and traditional programs.

A 2021 analysis of LinkedIn data on boot camp graduates by boot camp research and comparison search platform SwitchUp revealed that popular technical boot camp alumni have held positions at the big five technology companies.

From Wax Specialist to Programmer in Under a Year

Parris Athena had tried it all—actress, dancer, wax specialist. The Boston native did a stint in Los Angeles and tried her hand for a few years in auditions before returning home and landing a job as a wax specialist, earning just under $50,000 per year.

Athena jumpstarted her tech career just a few years ago after attending a hackathon she learned about upon visiting a presentation at her younger brother's school.

The boot camp offered a scholarship to their full-stack development course. After winning a slot in their program and the scholarship, she started training.

Six months later, she was offered a junior developer job working for a newly launched startup, almost doubling her salary to the tune of $80,000. Despite the company going defunct, she was able to quickly land a job at another startup, along with an even higher salary.

In Boston, which had a limited pool of Black and brown tech workers within the city and an even smaller option for diverse networking within the industry, Athena took to the internet looking for community.

It was on Twitter that she found a group of newly credentialed or aspiring Black techies seeking support, career advice, skills advice, and more. The open community and connections offered her much more than she could find in her native Boston. She desperately wanted to feel included within a space where few people look like her.

In December 2019, she introduced the hashtag #BlackTechTwitter into the Twittersphere. The hashtag quickly caught on, with thousands using the identifier to connect with each other to share career advice, job opportunities, and technical tips for projects they were working on, in real time.

Through the culmination of the hashtag, Athena was not only able to lead the cultivation of an online community but also demonstrated that help is everywhere you look, and sometimes creating the idea to find the support you are looking for can be just a click away.

This mirrors earlier subculture communities like #BlackTwitter, #LatinxTwitter, and other offshoots of cybercultures

(continued)

(*continued*)

following those of MySpace, AOL's Black Voices, Black Planet, and other covert digital gathering cyberspaces where nerds of color have gathered since the dawn of accessible internet to talk about everything from hip hop to programming languages.

Today, Athena's initiative has transformed into a formal community called Black Tech Pipeline. Through the platform, Black Tech Pipeline connects companies to Black technical talent and provides users access to mentors and more.

Learn more over at Blacktechpipeline.com.

Credentialing While Black or Brown

The nonrequirement of a four-year degree is not without its flaws—especially among historically excluded groups and communities hailing from lower-income neighborhoods or schools that are not your usual recruiting center for big tech companies. The credentialing decision might have to be taken with a grain of salt as you think through your own strategy for gaining a tech education. For many of us, myself included, the four-year degree definitely helped me to unlock a few doors. If you can score a college education without student debt, and a fast track to job opportunities, this can be a worthwhile time investment.

If you're offered a full-ride scholarship to a four-year university, is it worth your while? Absolutely. If you're able to work or participate in a co-op opportunity to work and learn on the job, is it worth it? Absolutely.

While not all programs are created equal, the opportunity for an alternative, as well as the deep connection to top companies for immediate job training and placement, can provide a healthy route to a good income for those interested in single-subject learning without all of the bloat of a traditional education.

Standard universities, state schools, and community colleges provide a plethora of options for returning professionals looking to train for new careers. Many have launched distinctive certification programs in partnership with top employers that match those of new boot camp offerings but provide them within an academic setting, offering flexibility for those who are already busy in their careers or need flexible schedules.

Historically Black Colleges and Universities have also made significant strides in the professional development space. Partnerships with corporate companies have led to the launch of training programs in high-growth industries like cybersecurity and data science.

The Atlanta University Center, which houses Spelman College, Morehouse College, and Clark Atlanta University, teamed up with United Health Care in 2019 to build out a data science curriculum course for incoming freshmen and sophomores. Google has worked with Howard University to provide training experiences and internships to a few hundred students within the university's computer science program. In the beginning of 2021, Google partnered with the Alpha Kappa Alpha sorority on its Grow with Google initiative to train 100,000 Black women in digital skills by 2022.

Capitalizing on offered programs, whether a traditional four-year program or training certificate, can be a foot in the door when leveraged strategically. Getting into tech and adjacent industries is about using what you have to get where you want. What you do with it is all part of the hustle.

More Than Just Tech

Tech industry companies still need to run other facets of the business. Not everyone has to be or wants to be someone who codes all day. Other aspects of running a successful company include hiring people with transferable skills. Thus, many are transitioning their skills from traditional environments and landing jobs within tech spaces in the same field but applying them to the world of software.

Companies also hire for roles in:

- Human resource management
- Operations management
- Sales
- Marketing
- Recruitment
- Account management
- Business development
- Quality assurance testing
- Customer support and help desk support

Workforce Development

Forward-thinking cities are also moving urgently to clean up long-standing issues related to economic mobility and communities of color who have historically been left behind. The line of demarcation between rising tech communities and opportunities to onboard local residents into the city's progress has consistently been a missing framework.

Despite their stellar growth of commerce shaped by hosting the world's top startups, cities like Seattle, New York City, San Jose, Los Angeles, San Francisco, and Washington, DC boast the highest rates of homelessness in the country.

As technology advances, growing inequality continues to rear its ugly head. Workforce development programs, which see billions in federal dollars in infrastructure funding, aren't always created equal.

In Charlotte, following various scathing studies of Mecklenburg County's lowest-ranking environment for economic mobility in 2015, particularly for a city that is one-third Black and is seeing a growing Hispanic population, several players got into the game of modeling training programs to help advance workforce development in new ways.

The Workforce Investment Network (WIN) program was designed as a pilot workforce development opportunity through the Carolina Fintech Hub and partners like Bank of America, Wells Fargo, and other major financial institutions. The offer? Twenty-four weeks of paid technical training, an apprenticeship within a local banking firm, and a junior-level position making at least $50,000 per year. One hundred students have cycled through the program, with several participants going from earning just $20,000 to now earning upwards of $90,000 after three years in the program.

Global nonprofit Goodwill Industries provides job training and reskilling in IT, banking, and health care services, training upwards of 125,000 people each year across its more than 3,000 centers across the country. The free training includes earning certifications in SQL server, CompTIA A+, and QA testing.

Check with your city, county, or state about what is available that could be a ticket to free training and direct connections to programs that can get you into a higher-paying job.

WORD BANK: Hackathon

Noun. An event in which a large number of people meet to engage in collaborative computer programming.

*"a series of 48-hour hackathons to build new web and mobile services"**

Where are they hosted?

Many companies will host hackathons open to the public to help work on a particular problem to think through new ideas and come up with potential solutions, software, or design ideas.

Why should I get involved?

Hackathons are great ways to meet other technologists or aspiring technologists within your city. They're also a great way to check out potential employers, meet recruiters, and build your network.

You can team up and some teams win cash prizes for their ideas to help implement. It's a great resume builder as well.

Source: Dictionary.com.

While not all programs are created equal, use the following guiding questions to help you determine if the program is right for you:

- Is the training paid or does it provide a stipend that enables you to cover your expenses (whether full or partial) so that you can properly plan for yourself or your family?
- Are there opportunities to connect with instructors or program leaders to help you determine if the program would be a good fit for your goals?
- Does the program have a timeline for completion, a helpful staff, a positive cohort of students?
- Does the program have a track record of placing people into full-time jobs?
- Whom does the program name as its key employers?
- Does the program offer any additional support services that would help you participate in the program? Do they offer services like child care, stipends, transportation support, computer devices, or other supports if you need them?

Case Study: Don't Go It Alone: Career Karma

Before he entered the technology industry, Ruben Harris was a professional cellist. He graduated from Southern Adventist University in 2010 on a music scholarship, double-majoring in music and business administration.

Though an artist at heart, Ruben's interest in business ushered him into the investment banking industry. But as he charted his path to success, it was the technology industry's lure that led him to pack his bags and make the move to San Francisco in 2014, where he joined a shared house community of hackers and tech enthusiasts as he navigated the open world of Silicon Valley.

(continued)

(continued)

The road wasn't linear. Ruben had to learn the language of the industry. He went on to complete several training certificates, including Computer Science 101. From there, he networked his way into circles, eventually landing jobs with companies like AltSchool and Honor, leading inside sales teams.

Along the way, Ruben began documenting his journey into technology. In 2017, with a group of friends (who became business partners), he launched the *Breaking Into Startups* podcast, interviewing people from all backgrounds on how they were able to land a career in tech after transitioning from an unrelated field. The program provided advice and program recommendations to listeners who were looking to make the transition or felt overwhelmed by exactly where to start.

The podcast turned out to be a lead driver to several boot camps, drawing new students to programs that hit Ruben up for formal partnerships for advertising. And that's when a new tool to help people wanting to break into tech was born.

Today, Ruben is the co-founder and CEO of Career Karma, a platform that has emerged as the dominant technical school and career advice platform helping over 1 million site visitors each month find their way through thousands of boot camps and professional development programs across the country.

The tool is designed to take the stress out of choosing the program with the right fit, tuition structure, and learning flexibility. All it takes is filling out a simple intake questionnaire, building a profile, getting matched to best-fitting programs, and preparing for the entrance application.

Career Karma adds additional layers with hosted orientations and an internal community hub that boasts nearly half a million users—mostly women and people of color looking for new opportunities and a shot at working and growing their earning potential within the technology industry.

The company names partners like Goodwill, several Oakland-based nonprofits, national GED programs, and various state workforce development programs that funnel their graduates onto the Career Karma platform.

Career Karma has successfully matched thousands of students to technical training programs, including students like Atlanta-based developer Kesha Lake.

Kesha, a proud wife and mother of two, works as a front-end engineer at a popular tech apparel company—a job that would have been out of reach had she not decided to take advantage of a certificate program.

Several attempts at earning a degree over the last 10 years had gone unfulfilled. Hailing from a Caribbean family who just wanted her to finish school and become a nurse, she turned to the Career Karma platform following a friend's advice to try her hand at a career in tech.

No one in her family had a tech background, but that didn't stop her from testing the waters. After three months in a full-stack software boot camp course, she

(continued)

> *(continued)*
>
> landed her first job earning a $98,000 annual salary, earning promotions along the way. Though her family was skeptical about Kesha's pivot at first, they quickly jumped on board, spreading the word throughout their family and church community about Kesha's success and the opportunities within the tech industry.

Action Items

- **Family meeting.** Set up a family discussion to talk about your ideas and strategies for advancing your education. Is everyone on the same page? Are there funds to cover expenses—not just tuition, but books, boarding if required, trips, and so on?
- **Career and salary search.** Research which careers you might be interested in and look up the corresponding salaries. Then determine how many of those jobs were available within your city. Who are the top employers? What is the education required and how long will it take?
- **Where the money resides.** Create a money strategy for reaching your goal. Find out if there are tuition reimbursement programs offered at your company. What about programs offered through unemployment assistance services? Are there scholarship opportunities you can leverage to lower the cost of your educational pursuit?
- **Determine your timeline.** Put a date on every goal. From scholarships to applications to orientations, use your digital or printed calendar and begin adding key deadlines to keep you on track. Then add the dates for when you want

to begin preparing for each deadline, whom you might need to help you review or proofread your applications, and what letters of reference or recommendations you might need as part of your application requirements. Your organization will pay off big time.

- **Research good fits.** Use online programs like Career Karma to help you navigate the matching process and get a listing of potential programs that might be a good fit for you. Or check out what is offered at your local community college or vocational programs. Speak with the counselors and other students of the program. Ask about placement rates and where they have been successful in placing students (which companies and how long it took).

- **Dip your toe in the water.** Spend $10 or a little more to take an introductory class on the topic you're thinking about signing up for. Programs like Udemy, edX, Skillshare, LinkedIn Learning, Lynda, and others offer introductory courses. Some boot camps even host hackathons to help you learn basic skills and give you a chance to meet instructors and learn more about their offerings.

- **What's free.99.** Research certificate program offerings at top tech companies and big employers to see if they have free or very-low-cost programs. See if they offer scholarships, how to get into the programs, how long they take, and if they provide access to additional job opportunities or training. Try a local nonprofit like Goodwill, which provides access to free training both in person and online.

4

Don't Let the Robots Scare You

The robots are already here. And they've been with us for a while now.

THEY'RE THE NEW checkout stand. The bank teller. The vacuum cleaner in our homes. The devices that turn the water off and on in public restrooms. They power our cars and even manage our money. They've lived among us for quite some time as complementary efficiencies to our lives, and we expect them to do some of the mindless chores we are no longer interested in doing ourselves. They don't have faces or names or families, but they are integrated into the most intimate parts of our lives.

The myth about the world ending and robots taking over is very much something you might find in a Hollywood storyline on a forgotten-about Netflix watch list. Instead, interdependency, where humans and machines work to execute tasks together, is what will allow us to focus on bigger tasks while letting automation do the repetitive work we would rather not do ourselves.

So what does this mean for us in terms of how we navigate a robot present and future? Learning how to fix, train, or work with these robots is where we would do well to focus our efforts and our time.

Technology has fundamentally changed the way in which we live and work, there is no doubt about it. And with its presence comes great opportunity and the responsibility to learn from our existing spaces to determine how we can leverage these technologies to create greater efficiencies within our lives and also adopt their usage in how we think about designing our futures.

The goal of technology is to remove some of the difficult and laborious tasks from humans and pass them off to computers so that humans can spend more time building new things and doing more meaningful work.

But, like most evolutions, the impact on various communities can be quite debilitating. In this chapter, we'll discuss the impact of automation on communities of color, and ways in which to begin mitigating some of these challenges.

WORD BANK: Upskilling

To acquire more advanced skills through additional education and training.

Source: Merriam Webster.

Automation and the Impact on Communities of Color

Automation

At its core, automation is about implementing a system to complete repetitive, easily replicated tasks without the need for human labor.

Instead, humans can focus their time and energy on much harder problems and decision-making.

McKinsey released its first report on automation and its impact on Black and Latinx communities in 2019. The study showed that many of the jobs where these groups were overrepresented were service-oriented jobs like restaurant workers, cashiers, servers, home health aides, and other roles that are low-wage or at risk for automation.

With these jobs quickly being impacted or replaced by computers in some aspect, the value of these jobs, typically lower-paying, would be at risk within the next 20 years as computers become smarter and employers prioritize knowledge work over traditional manual labor and services.

The jobs of the 1980s and 1990s that launched Black people like my grandfather into the middle class without the need for very much formal education have all but disappeared. The economic climate of today is not filled with pension plans, employers that will provide sick leave or maternity leave, or health care coverage. Unfortunately, unlike most developed nations, the U.S. ranks all but last on the scale for supportive services to enable thriving quality of living environments, particularly for those at the bottom of the economic base.

But don't let the data fool you or your potential narrative. As there are some rooted challenges, during this time more than ever, Black Americans and Latinx Americans are attending college at a much higher rate. There is greater access to training opportunities online and through the country's largest employers, often for free (as you can see in our previous chapter on preparing for a job in the future of work).

Reskilling, or the urgency of teaching new skills in the world of work, isn't limited to communities of color.

Employers are even identifying ways in which they can own the responsibility of training their employees for the skills they'll need to become better and more successful at their jobs. Employers are now making commitments of millions of dollars to take responsibility and invest in training up their own employees into the jobs that will be needed as automation changes the nature of work.

Case Study: Reskilling America

Many of the jobs that exist today did not exist a decade ago. And we remain in an ever-changing landscape where the nature of work requires an outlook on a future that hasn't yet defined itself.

We have seen jobs disappear in droves. From coal mining to parking lot attendants, jobs that were once able to help feed families no longer exist, and in the wake of the changeover, this puts communities at risk.

Thus the push for upskilling and rapidly reskilling people for the jobs of the future. While many are working to tackle this, a few platforms have found unique ways to provide training and support new ways in order to get people hired or to remove barriers for them getting hired.

BlueStudios

This is a virtual platform teaching STEM skills to students from kindergarten through 12th grade. Classes are taught by a variety of educators from all backgrounds. They're offered both live and on-demand. One-on-one coaching, STEM kits, and other teaching tools help bring the education right into your home.

ChargerHelp

This company works with workforce development programs and organizations to train and hire people to fix and maintain the software that runs electric vehicle (EV) charging stations. With service providers around the country, they certify technicians and hire them as full-time employees to serve customers building EV infra-structure in cities across the country.

RC3

The R3 Score background check platform changes how we view those with criminal backgrounds, giving people a fair shot of defining their lives, not by a past decision but by where they are now. Using systems like the Fair Credit Reporting Act (FCRA), the scoring method provides two unique scores that contextualize criminal histories and credit scores. For instance, the scoring method provides details on whether an individual received a certification in prison, shares the severity of the offense, and how long ago the offense was. From a credit perspective, it provides additional data points on how an individual spends. In short, wherever assessments and background checks are required, RC3 can be used.

Removing Coded Bias by Becoming Builders

The downside of the technology being built today is that it is not without its biases. When the majority of our technology and software systems have been developed by homogeneous groups, the coded bias that exists in the wild and is embedded in the framework by humans becomes embedded in the technology we're increasingly relying on. But there are detrimental consequences to introducing technology that is missing key cultural competencies.

Case Study: Dr. Ruha Benjamin

Dr. Ruha Benjamin is a professor of African American studies at Princeton University, founding director of the IDA B. WELLS Just Data Lab, and author of *People's Science* and *Race After Technology*.

In her examination of everyday apps to complex algorithms, Benjamin works to help audiences understand how existing and emerging technologies can deepen social inequities and reinforce white supremacy, calling this phenomenon of encoded bias "the New Jim Code."

She warns that technology has the potential to deepen discrimination, masking itself behind an autonomous and neutral framework while hiding or amplifying social division, racial hierarchies, and furthering social injustices in everyday life.

Take for instance how racial profiling of Black and Latinx people leads to higher rates of arrests in these communities. Benjamin argues that the police data that trains the algorithms and machine learning tools that make predictions about future crimes will negatively impact these communities, as the overrepresentation in the data can falsely predict who's seen to be at a higher risk for committing a crime.

But Benjamin doesn't believe that simply adding more diverse groups to the tech industry will solve these long-standing and impending issues, especially not when certain groups might be disempowered to challenge discriminatory behaviors or put themselves at risk for job loss when seeking to address inequality. Instead, she argues, an overhaul of practices and how technology is designed must be addressed.

In 2020, police officers arrested Robert Julian-Borchak Williams on his front lawn in Farmington Hills, Michigan, in front of his toddler children for a crime that facial recognition software said he committed. After being detained for 30 hours and released on bail, at his follow-up hearing Wayne County prosecutors dropped the charges due to insufficient evidence. The facial recognition software used by Michigan State Police had misidentified a thief who took off with over $3,800 worth of jewelry from a retail store some 25 miles south in Detroit. The image was grainy at best, only showing the shadowy image of a nondistinctive Black man.

Dr. Joy Buolamwini, a notable algorithmic justice researcher, told NPR in an interview about the case that the mismatch presented just one of many dangers facial recognition technology posed to people of color.

In her research at MIT, Buolamwini brought to light the flaws in how facial recognition technology does a poor job at identifying dark skin or female facial structures. In order for the software she was testing to recognize her, she had to wear a white mask. Her work since then has been advocating for the governance of algorithms to be improved and regulated as these particular technologies continue to make their way into police systems and facial recognition technology that is often flawed and has led to wrongful arrests of Black people.

WORD BANK: Facial Recognition Technology

A software system that matches a human face from a digital image or video against a database of faces to ID and measures the features of a given image.

(continued)

(*continued*)

You might be most familiar with this technology if you have a mobile device. Most modern smartphones today unlock through tools like the Apple iPhone Face ID or other facial recognition formats.

New York City successfully banned facial recognition technology from its schools in 2020. Parents and privacy advocates sued the State Education Department for using the technology in a local school in an attempt to monitor student activity to help curb the rise in school shootings. Many states, considering the technology's inherent flaws and public concern for privacy, ban it from use in public spaces.

Other ways in which technology harms through its inherent biases are outlined by Dr. Cathy O'Neil in her book *Weapons of Math Destruction*, in which she shares how robots have determined who is creditworthy and who isn't, or how what types of ads we receive are based on an algorithm that might market one product to us over another.

Facebook was sued in 2019 by the U.S. Department of Housing and Urban Development. Their crime? Engaging in discriminatory housing practices by allowing advertisers to restrict who was allowed to see their ads through the social network's ads platform. Advertisers were able to filter out potential audience targets by race, religion, and national origin. So if a luxury apartment complex decides it does not wish to rent to or sell to a person of color or a person of any "other" kind of background, the filters and segmentation offered by Facebook's platform would allow for the discriminatory behavior to take place. In effect, these practices violate the federal Fair Housing Act of 1968 put in place to protect against the type of redlining familiar in the early and mid-1900s until the late 1960s. This form of artificial redlining had also been the center of a 2016 investigative report from news publisher ProPublica, who took Facebook's ad platform to task. They were successful in applying ad-targeting filters to exclude specific ethnic groups from seeing ads. If left unchecked, life in virtual spaces will continue to call for scrutiny, as well as regulation.

The need for technology to be developed and constructed and examined by diverse groups of technologists, leaders, scientists, and even social workers will define much of how we address the future of where technology expands from the present to the future. Mitigating harm, bias, and harmful impacts on vulnerable people, communities, and populations is also critical for an increasing technical future.

Despite the challenges, there is some change and hope on the horizon. Trends in pairing social work, artificial intelligence, and other fast-growing technologies are emerging.

Dr. Courtney Cogburn, associate professor of social work at Columbia University, created the 1000 Cut Journey in 2018. The immersive virtual reality experience allowed users to experience racism through a series of virtual experiences developed in collaboration with the Virtual Human Interaction Lab at Stanford University.

At the Data Science Institute, Dr. Cogburn conducts research on emerging technologies, including computational social science, to examine patterns and psychosocial effects of cultural racism and how virtual reality experiences can lead to changes in attitudes, social perception, and engagement (such as empathy, racial bias, structural competence, and behavior).

In his work as a dean and professor at Columbia University, Dr. Desmond Patton leads diversity, equity, and inclusion as director of research initiatives at the Data Science Institute, building tools for social media monitoring of violence in communities of color and regularly hosting discussions on responsible tech and ethics in communities of color.

A slow and steady expansion of ethics and equity curricula is reaching the classroom of future computer scientists and engineers in an effort to reduce bias and help train technologists to design inclusively and thoughtfully as they enter industries and build for technologies that haven't even been invented yet.

Cogburn and Patton introduced a course program at Columbia in 2019 for social work students to bridge the gap between their industry and the technology industry. Course work includes classes titled "Introduction to Emergent Technology, Media, and Society"; "Hacking for Social Impact"; "Data Science and Public Policy"; and "Statistical Thinking with Python Lab." The program also paired students with internships at companies like Facebook and Google.

Other institutions have been working toward humanizing technology for emerging engineers and other technology-centered majors across their institutions as of late. The Massachusetts Institute of Technology, Harvard, Stanford, and Georgetown boast recently introduced coursework aimed at teaching ethics to engineering students across a variety of disciplines.

If this trend continues across all major institutions and professional learning programs, the tide could turn for how new and advanced technologies are built with people from diverse backgrounds and perspectives in mind.

Beyond race, technology bias also shows up in how things are built when there aren't many women in the room to represent what life is like and to be involved in making decisions about what is being built. Take, for instance, the early iterations of health tracking apps that forgot to include options for logging periods or menstruation data.

In 2018, Amazon was forced to shut down its artificially intelligent hiring tool that mistakenly showed a bias against female applicants. According to Reuters, the team had been building computer programs since 2014 to review job applicants' resumes with the aim of mechanizing the search for top talent. But just a year later, the team recognized that the new system was not rating candidates for software developer and other technical jobs in a gender-neutral way.

The data was skewed. To build the system, Amazon had used 10-year-old data, based on the resumes of past employees, who were mostly male. The system taught itself that men were more qualified and preferred over female applicants. Resumes that had identifiers like "women's chess club" were categorized negatively and instantly downgraded.

In the effort to centralize and automate its hiring practices, the experiment flopped, and eventually, the team was disbanded. This particular case points to a much larger one around the limitations of machine learning and how far we have to go in understanding our relationship with technology as we attempt to integrate it into our lives more and more.

Why does all of this matter in the realm of our relationship with technology? It provides us a call to action to become builders and not just consumers of the world of technology.

Progress and advancement will happen, especially as we continue to compete on a global scale. Robots enable us to get smarter, work faster, build efficiently, and use technology to our advantage without forsaking our ethics or our commitment to community and access.

In fact, Black and brown entrepreneurs are building tech-enabled businesses that are helping to address true innovation opportunities within the least served communities and allowing the robots to do the dirty work while building lucrative businesses. You'll also read more about this in the chapter on ownership and entrepreneurship.

Working with the Robots

In the 1980s, Su Sanni's uncle made his living driving dollar vans that shuffled residents around the Jamaica, Queens, New York community to the nearest subway or bus stop. By the early 2000s, he was running a full-fledged transportation business.

The dollar van had long since been a staple of New York's Caribbean and Asian immigrant communities operating "shadow" transit services that ran $1 to $2 per passenger and solved the "last mile" problem for communities and neighborhoods that are typically underserved by local transportation options.

Before technology transformed the way in which we share a ride with strangers, the dollar van was a lifeline for those who lived too far from the nearest bus, rail, or subway stop and had few options outside of walking in any type of weather condition to get to work, school, and everyday appointments.

Seeing the transition of technology powering, and having apprenticed with his uncle in his younger years, Sanni founded the company Dollaride in 2017. Through its app, Dollaride offers vehicle operators a comprehensive dashboard to help them manage their business from operating their fleet to payment collection to connecting with riders looking to hail a van. Providing a tool for analysis and transparency, managers are able to determine the best routes, identify new route opportunities and expansion, track earnings, and manage compliance with local authorities.

During the start of the 2020 COVID-19 pandemic, Dollaride was positioned to help support residents deemed essential workers get to and from work when local transit was shut down or running at significantly reduced schedules. They even partnered with airport companies and services to create direct transportation for airport workers, especially those working the graveyard shift, to get from their jobs at the airport and safely and quickly to their homes.

With sights set on expansion to communities like Los Angeles, Miami, and other territories, Dollaride is just one example of complementary technology built around human experiences to make the everyday seamless and accessible no matter what neighborhood you're looking to get around in.

Other technology-enabled platforms facilitating economic mobility and solving challenges within communities are companies like ShearShare, Sizzors, and Squire, which, like Dollaride, provide platforms for the service industry of hairstylists and barbers to match with, find, and book clients through the use of their platforms.

Given that robots will likely not be the ones cutting our hair, painting our nails, or waxing our bodies, technology will continue to enable greater efficiencies within the market and provide greater access for the exchange of money.

The other side is also the delivery of information. During the pandemic, ShearShare was able to offer additional support services and advice on sanitization to help keep everyone safe.

Our homes, much like what was predeveloped in the Microsoft home I experienced during my days as an intern, are also access points for our ease of use with technology. Security cameras keep an eye on deliveries and guests. Devices that set ideal temperatures and can be controlled with our smartphones help us to monitor energy consumption.

A Remote Future

The global coronavirus pandemic accelerated a future of remote and virtual work that was already on the horizon. In almost an instant, we found ourselves logging into Zoom calls and meetings regularly, greeting our coworkers, doctors, and their kids and pets.

The move to remote work, or a hybrid of both home and the office, is drastically changing our relationship to work as well as our cities. Some of the benefits include decreased or no commutes, which saves time and money, and the ability to stay home and be present with family when possible without having to be at the office for long periods of time. Benefits are also expanding across critical social experiences in the growing remote workforce. Some of them are also psychological. In a *New York Times* article on the return to work, Black women tech workers talked about the easing of anxiety they felt from not having to deal with microaggressions at work. For some, particularly those with children, caregivers, those living and working with disabilities, or other physical and emotional considerations, the ability to earn a high salary and live and work from anywhere also offers its advantages with flexible work schedules or more accommodating home environments that might not be addressed in a traditional office.

Companies like SpaceX, Facebook, Google, Slack, and others created policies that enable working from home a few days a week as a permanent company policy following months out of the office during the pandemic. To keep up with the competition, other tech companies are following suit, providing greater flexibility to work completely remotely, opening the door to greater job prospects outside of workers' immediate geographic location.

Where to Get Skilled Up

We don't have to be afraid of the robots—we just need to know how to work with them, and for those of us who want to train, we need to learn how to build them as well. No matter what our interest is in this space, having a working knowledge of the technology that is shaping jobs, money, education, and a host of other aspects of our daily lives will put us at an advantage as we begin to consider how we want to use our talents and skills for a rapidly changing environment.

Workforce development programs are more critical than ever and can provide a host of options and opportunities for accessing free training and even paid training for those looking to add to their skills or training in a new industry. In Chapter 3 we talked about a few critical places where you can access training, as big tech companies provide online certifications and programs as well as access to potential employers.

On our site at upperhandbook.com, I share a list of conferences, training programs, and resources to help you navigate environments where you can continue to learn and grow your skills.

When working with groups and consulting for cities and private sector clients on how to help navigate the future of

work, the biggest barrier to getting started was not know-
ing where information was. I get it—the technology sector
can be highly intimidating, which is why this book exists,
but more importantly, the information is available and will
continue to be updated online and crowdsourced to help you
navigate opportunities.

You'll be able to search the interactive map to find programs in your region or find national programs you can par-
take in online.

Following is a list of easy-access learning environments
that offer training, on-demand learning, and resources to
help you get started. Many of these programs are no- to low-
cost and can be done from home.

Upskilling Learning Environments

Your Local Library

The library is a haven for classes, literature, and entertainment that is already paid for with taxes. Whether you
need a basic computer literacy class, want to learn website design or the Google Suite or Microsoft applications,
instruction sometimes offered both online and in-person,
it serves as a great place in your local community to get
acclimated to basic tools.

LinkedIn Learning

Associated with the social media platform for professional
networking, LinkedIn Learning provides a series of video
courses taught by industry experts in software, business,
and creative fields.

SkillShare

The project-based learning platform is also offered online and focuses not just on providing lectures and information on topic-based training, but also helps you build up a portfolio of work upon completing assignments.

Udemy

With classes ranging from marketing to management to programming, Udemy's online marketplace provides courses from experts for both students and professionals.

Your Local Community College and University

Over 40,000 unique programs are offered online through schools with online courses and certificate programs. Academic-based programs can also offer formal certificates for their programs.

5

Money Talks

I LEFT TENS of thousands of dollars on the table when I landed my first role at a new startup company.

After we'd agreed upon my salary (which I'd failed to negotiate), the company offered me stock options. It was the first time ever in my career that I'd been offered equity, and while I understood that it meant I'd have a relatively small ownership stake in the business as I helped to grow it, I was truly out of my depth as to what that looked like from a compensation perspective.

My family was a family of pension plans and 401(k)-matching programs. We were not a stocks-and-bonds or investment strategy–driven family. My peers and friends from undergrad were working for startups of a different sort—having also never experienced being offered equity as part of their total financial package. So my understanding of the equity offer was limited to what I could find on Google, and with the urgency to onboard me as quickly as possible, I said yes to what ultimately reduced my ability to put that forsaken money into long-term wealth-building tools.

As co-workers whispered about the possibility of the company going public as early as the following year, and discussions about what they'd do with their newfound riches arose, I sat silently at my desk, embarrassed that I'd played the game entirely wrong.

I was college-educated, had read the books by several financial gurus, but when it came to understanding the mechanics of the tech world and its financial structure, there wasn't much information I could access to navigate my early days as an employee. Years later, when the company eventually did go public, my shares, which I purchased with the last of my savings and a contribution from my mom, were paltry slices compared to those of my peers, who had, like me, since moved on. It was a hard lesson to learn. And despite having a few connections in tech, having an open money conversation just wasn't a common practice for me.

Silicon Valley, the cluster of cities and technology communities across the San Francisco Bay Area that boast elite school engineer dropouts and investment firms that have spun out companies like Google, Apple, Oracle, and others, has been defining the tech landscape over the last 30 years. Cities looking to be seen as emerging hubs for innovation often refer to themselves as "the next Silicon Valley" or the "Silicon Valley of the South" or adopt some form of a nickname like New York City's "Silicon Alley."

A scripted comedy series on HBO, released in 2014, with the same name, followed a group of computer programmers in the 1980s to Silicon Valley as they attempted to get rich in the high-tech gold rush that marked the time.

Startup, released in 2016, became a fan favorite when its three-season run was added to Netflix in early 2021. The drama followed three unlikely partners as they face tremendous obstacles to bring their new digital currency to the market.

The bubble of the San Francisco, Palo Alto, and Mountain View environment has been promising early success for young professionals and those of that ilk willing to wear the T-shirt and commit the necessary time to see a company take off since the dot-com era of the 1990s made everyone feel like they were playing a role in the future.

Many Silicon Valley millionaires are made as a result of discounted stocks and bonus stock earned through their years of employment at successful companies that eventually go public or get acquired. The average salary for an entry-level computer engineer in Silicon Valley fresh out of college is between $88,000 and $98,000. Those aren't small potatoes for a 20-something who may have very few responsibilities.

SIDEBAR: Startups, of course, aren't the only game in town. Stability in salary and benefits also comes from the biggest and longest players in the game with big employee bases, including companies like Boeing, IBM, Duke Energy, financial institutions, and others that are also aggressively recruiting tech talent.

Understanding where the jobs are, where they are going, and what they pay is critical knowledge we have to acquire as we carve paths for ourselves and our families to set up long-term wealth-building opportunities throughout our careers. This knowledge is becoming much more accessible as discussions of salary and what it takes to get into the tech industry have made their way on social media.

More important is understanding how the industry works and developing the necessary networks and social groups to learn from. I should have spent more time asking hard questions instead of forfeiting my compensation due to lack of knowledge. If someone from my background and education missed the boat, what does it mean for others with little to no social resources they can tap to help equip them for defining and determining their financial career path and future?

WORD BANK: Vesting

Whether it be employee stock options or a 401(k) retirement plan, most employers require a certain amount of time for you to be working at their company before you officially "vest" and can take advantage of these benefits over a period of time.

For instance, if you vest one year over a four-year vesting schedule, you will earn the ability to keep 25 percent of your stock options once you hit the one-year mark.

Starting at Home

My failure to negotiate a better salary and the stock options offered to me was a symptom of a much larger issue. My network had been limited to a peer group and mentor group of people who had never worked for startup tech companies that offered equity as part of an employment package. Also, having money conversations wasn't exactly a common practice in my household.

My family, to this day, does not discuss money openly. It's taboo. There are no dinner-table discussions about it. The only advice from a group of hard-working Midwest folks I received growing up is that you save your money, pay your bills on time, and take your one or two vacations each year. There was always enough, but a strategy on how things were acquired for long-term wealth-building was never on the agenda. *Investing* wasn't a word that floated around family holidays. Our investment was in our community, political advocacy, and our social affairs.

The only regular money experience I can remember was watching Mom pay bills at the dining room table on Sunday afternoons. Before online banking was a thing, she'd sit at the smooth cherry-wood table with a glass of Vernor's ginger ale, the phone speaker volume turned up, recording the check numbers spoken by the electronic bank teller and scribbling in her checkbook which expenditures had cleared her account.

When Grandpa or any extended family member slid me a crisp $20 bill, that money went right into my personal piggy bank until Mom took me down to the Boeing Employees Credit Union to open a kid's savings account.

I was around six years old when the bank teller slid a white booklet with the slogan "saving is fun" printed in Crayon-like ink on the front over to me from across the counter. I was too short to look her in the face, but I thanked her for the booklet and let my mom escort me to a table on the side to write my name in big letters. It was an account of my own where mom said I could put all the money from my piggy bank in. Mom helped me count the dollars and coins I'd collected from birthdays and holidays. She helped me record the final dollar amount on my deposit booklet and fill out a slip of paper she then handed to the teller along with my money.

Mom treated my having a bank account as a big deal. I was less than thrilled. If it were up to me, my dollars and coins would have been just fine sitting in my pencil-shaped bank comfortably on my bedroom desk. She clearly had a master plan that went far beyond my understanding. As she handed over my little treasure, I made mental lists of all the things I could buy with that money at the Imagineer store or local Toys "R" Us.

Soon, my little savings account grew. Money from chores, babysitting, working in the salon, teaching dance, or assisting Mom at the office was added to the account. "Keep saving" was the only financial advice I received. And, like most teenagers, I rebelled. As my deposit booklet noted my good fortune, I wanted to do anything but save. There were shoes to buy, clothes to shop for, magazines, gadgets, and other meaningless items that were so very important to me at the time. Asking for permission to spend my hard-earned money on those things felt like hell.

Mom let me spend, but she focused my attention on bills, not more useless items—specifically, the bills I was creating that far exceeded her budget. As my side hustles returned more dollars to my account, I began paying for my own dance classes, dance shoes, and extracurricular activities that went beyond the initial planned budget.

Money earned during my summer internships was also tossed into my arbitrary savings account, with a percentage donated back to TAF to pour back into all they had poured into me. After my first summer interning, I'd saved a little over $1,000 of my earnings in a non-interest-bearing account, with the voice of Mom in my head reminding me that money was supposed to be there for that fateful day that "I would need it." I loosely decided that the money would help me with college expenses—the ones my peers who had gone off to college a year or so ahead of me warned were shock expenses like $300 textbooks and technology fees.

Like most students coming from a single-parent household, I knew that I'd be responsible for aiding in some way to reduce the cost of college, be that through hustling for scholarships or working part-time while attending classes.

This experience was starkly different from that of some of the peers I'd met within my high school internship experiences who hailed from wealthy families. Their college tuition had already been planned and paid for well before they were born. Heading into my senior year of high school one summer, I sat at lunch with the other interns, who decided to meet up for tea at a nearby Japanese restaurant.

One intern, who had completed high school at the nearby all-girls private school, was headed into her freshman year on a full ride to the University of Washington. She told us that her parents had saved nearly $150,000 for her education. Considering the scholarship she'd earned, they were gifting her the no-longer-necessary tuition money for her to use to purchase a home. She gleefully spoke about not having to live in the dorms and being excited to purchase a new car. Her father? A CEO of a major tech company who flew around the world so much that he had enough mileage points for her entire family of five to fly around the world at least twice in first class. She shared her life story not to gloat, but as a passing comment, assuming everyone had similar circumstances. We did not. In fact, not a single one of us could relate to a life that did not require some level of struggle, even if we had parents who owned homes and did okay.

Meeting at intern orientation day, you could immediately sniff out the class divides, and we spoke about them frequently among our groups. Though we had all landed at the same place within a world-class software company, our backgrounds and various class levels meant that how we experienced spaces was not of the same caliber.

I'll never forget sitting down to lunch at Microsoft with my friend and fellow TAF classmate Aubrielle during our summer high school internship. That particular day we were discussing our individual school experiences. She'd been attending the same private high school as Bill Gates. She was one of few Black people attending one of the top schools in the city. Tuition was paid partially through a scholarship and the rest from her father, who was a pastor.

Aubrielle had a stellar education, but a very limited social network. Where her peers' parents were nuclear scientists, doctors, attorneys, and professional scientists and engineers, those professions weren't always relevant to the day-to-day school curriculum of advanced mathematics and sciences. At lunch that day, Aubrielle shared that something as mundane as completing homework revealed a disparity between her and her peers. Her friends' parents worked in industries that were relevant to the coursework. By default, they had consistent exposure to industries and information that she had to search for. Their families talked about money, because they had it, and how to navigate the spectrum of college and career options in a way that wasn't readily present in her immediate home environment. I could relate.

The family plan for me to attend college was predetermined by sheer social expectation, but not a strategy. There was no college savings account waiting for me upon my high school graduation. And despite having earned several scholarships, they wouldn't be enough to cover my out-of-state tuition fees. By choice, I ditched staying home and attending the local university, assuming I'd be able to pay back my student loans after graduation, delaying the debt as much as possible, because that's what I saw others in our social circle do. Student loans were just a part of life. Everyone, it seems, had them. There had been no specific strategy discussed at our dinner table on how to make college work financially, how to pick the best major, or even what taking on loans would mean for my long-term financial future. The wishful thinking, without a surefire strategic approach to my education or a solid spending plan, would prove to be one of the greatest financial barriers to wealth building I'd face—and, with millions of my peers, is a lesson I wish I could have the option to relearn.

The State of Affairs

I didn't begin my foray into investing in the stock market until my mid-20s. Despite feeling like a very late bloomer, compared to my peers in tech, being invested in the stock market largely correlates with your race, class, income, and age. Some of this attitude might be attributed to the fears of the stock market crash of 2008, just when many of us were completing our undergraduate education and launching into a nonexistent job market, or watching as many people our parents' age saw their 401(k) savings cut in half or lose a ridiculous amount of money.

According to an analysis by Pew Research, more than half of Americans are invested in the stock market, although white families are more likely to be invested in the stock market than are Black and Hispanic families.

Based on the data, 61 percent of white households own some stock, compared to 31 percent of Black households and 28 percent of Hispanic households. Amounts invested are also points of difference where the median invested for white households is $51,000, compared to $12,000 for Black families, and under $11,000 for Hispanic families.

The market has always been obscure and scary when you've been an outsider and not well-versed on the topic before you're thrust into a job that forces you to choose health plans, insurance plans, and retirement benefits with key terms that you're unaware of. There aren't any classes or courses in high school that teach you about tax strategies, investing, saving, retirement planning, or how to buy proper insurance.

The national economy has certainly taken us for a ride. I know folks hate when millennials whine about how bad we have it, but it took over a decade just to get back to ground zero. We were sold a bill of goods in job markets that weren't similar to what our parents had been afforded. College expenses outpaced the actual return on investment. The cost of living in major cities rose sharply. And despite technology unlocking doors to advancement, the gig economy exacerbated an era of shifts where everyone works but no one has any stability.

Take on a decade of economic uncertainty, and millennials—myself included—have had to make harsh choices. We're less likely to purchase homes or have children. We're getting married later in life, and the stability of our financial futures continues to wane following various economic catastrophes that have stunted our growth.

There are also the realities of what economists, scholars, and analysts refer to as the racial wealth gap. Examinations of net worth among various racial groups in a 2019 Survey of Consumer Finances by the Federal Reserve note that the median and mean asset values of an average white family stand at $188,200 and $983,400, respectively. For other racial groups, this number is significantly lower, representing a stark concentration of wealth among one primary group.

MEDIAN NET WORTH (in thousands)	
White	$188.2
Black	$24.1
Hispanic	$36.1
Other	$74.5

MEAN NET WORTH (in thousands)	
White	$983.4
Black	$142.5
Hispanic	$165.5
Other	$657.2

Source: Federal Reserve 2019 Survey of Consumer Finances.

Small gains in wealth increases through the years earned between 2013 and 2016 have all but vanished as a consequence of the pandemic as families faced job losses, evictions, the shuttering of businesses, caregiving responsibilities, and other losses of income.

Many factors play a role in these long-standing disparities, like 246 years of chattel slavery, discriminatory laws and policies during the Jim Crow era preventing Black access to job opportunities and full participation in public life, the GI Bills that provided education assistance and housing support for returning white veterans but not Black ones, redlining and discriminatory home lending practices, and the destruction of thriving Black communities like Tulsa, Oklahoma, and Durham's Black Wall Street in the 1920s.

Income gaps also spell disparity in total household income that could be leveraged to grow assets but is missing when accounted for race and gender. The Gender Pay Gap Report for 2021 by PayScale.com showed that women overall earned just 82 cents for every $1 a white man earned. Broken down by race and gender, the numbers are much more scathing.

WEALTH GAP BY GENDER/RACE

	Women	Men
White	$0.82	$1.00
Asian	$0.85	$1.15
Black	$0.63	$0.87
Hispanic or Latinx	$0.55	$0.91
Native American	$0.60	$0.91

Source: U.S. Census Bureau, PayScale *Gender Pay Gap Report,* National Partnership for Working Families, Pew Research.

Controlling for education, occupation, and years of experience, gaps persist. Lost wages over a 40-year career means that a woman or man of color has fewer earnings being used strategically for wealth-building over the course of their lifetime.

In its 2018 report *Automation and the African American Workforce*, McKinsey warned that African Americans and Latinx workers are overrepresented in occupations at the lower end of the pay scale and are most likely to be affected by automation.

Job losses during the 2020 pandemic were highest in areas likely to be transformed by technology, such as food services, production work, office support, and other retail environments that weren't able to be performed remotely. Disproportionately, the pandemic pushed Black and Latinx employees out of employment compared to white workers.

The net impacts of the COVID-19 pandemic on total wages across racial groups have yet to be seen.

Income challenges aside, one of the largest factors at play is that white families receive larger inheritances compared to other racial groups. Intergenerational transfers of homes and other monetary assets protect families against uncontrollable factors such as job loss or other disruptions in income. It also means having access to high-quality housing in better-resourced neighborhoods with more well-funded schools, and greater options of routes to higher education and strong employment opportunities.

Federal Reserve research also revealed that white families have greater access to tax-sheltered savings plans and investment resources and decisions that aid in the accumulation of wealth and financial stability and security.

Kicking Things into Gear

Despite the harsh statistics, there's a game to be played by leveraging data to understand where and how certain industries providing greater pay equity and career-long earning potential can help narrow the gap.

According to PayScale's analysis, technology, engineering, and science jobs achieve the highest level of pay equity, when controlling for compensable factors. While the representation of women and people of color within these industries is still lacking, the opportunity to train for the industries and jobs of the future requires developing a strategic game plan to arm ourselves with not just tech skills but also soft skills, like increasing our negotiation skills during salary discussions and asking for promotions more often, which can help to significantly impact our earning potential. Deepening our social networks also requires a strategic approach as getting access to a new job opportunity that might not be posted but comes as the result of a referral by a colleague or network contact.

Technology Access Game Plan

The average Silicon Valley engineer takes home $133,000 per year. But engineering salaries aren't the only ones to pay attention to when it comes to accessing high-paying careers within the tech industry. For those who are nontechnical, roles within marketing, human resources, sales, and operations are also up for grabs and are part of the core functions of any business that are in demand at existing and emerging technology companies.

These salaries, as you'll see in Chapter 10 when we discuss the jobs that are leading the future, can range from $75,000 to $150,000 annually along with benefits beyond standard health, vision, and dental insurance. To improve diversity, employee retention, and solve for a number of barriers that can prevent families, women, and other underrepresented groups from staying in their careers, tech companies are increasingly doubling down on generous benefits, including parental leave policies that can provide a paycheck for up to six months. Some companies provide a stipend to help with childcare costs; some even cover the costs of egg freezing and storage for those who'd like to delay family planning but hope to have control of their options in the future.

Not to mention that, before the pandemic, catered meals and well-stocked kitchens full of free food were a staple at big tech offices.

Believe it or not, there was a story in 2015 about one Google employee, a 23-year-old software engineer, who lived in a 128-square-foot truck outside of Google's offices in Mountain View, California. Considering the high cost of living in the city where he paid upward of $2,000 per month as an intern living in corporate housing, this employee decided to purchase a truck for $10,000, save 90 percent of his income to pay off his student loans, and spend his money exploring the city. He showered at the campus gym and ate three meals a day courtesy of the open kitchen. According to his blog, he's still living in the truck, debt-free.

Other over-the-top stories and extreme examples of technologists hacking their lives with unconventional routes to financial security include a 28-year-old software engineer who, during the pandemic, revealed on Twitter that she worked as many as three different tech jobs, lived in a van she converted and traveled the country—all the while bringing home $300,000 annually!

WORD BANK: Signing Bonus

Well-established technology companies often use signing bonuses to make a total compensation package attractive to prospective job candidates. This financial reward is offered by the company, in addition to other perks like moving expenses should a candidate need to relocate, in addition to base salary, bonuses, and other perks, and usually doesn't have to be paid back after a certain amount of time employed by the company.

And still, the power is in the options, such as being able to purchase stock at a discount and having the opportunity to benefit from being an early employee or earning much more than it would take to work 20-plus years to hit the million-dollars-in-assets goal so many of us have.

Not everyone working in these spaces has a traditional four-year degree. Many are self-taught. Some work in non-technical roles within technology companies. Some hail from community colleges, trade programs, or earned a certificate. Startups represent just one small portion of the employment opportunities within technology. For instance, the government has long been an employer of Black people within the IT and technology spaces and is usually a large employer of small and mid-size cities that have few enterprise companies.

Long term, the option to work remotely for well-funded and high-earning companies has increased exponentially, presenting one of the greatest times in our economic history to earn more, build wealth, and change the wealth trajectory of our families.

Accessible Wealth Building

Controlling our income and earning potential is both art and science. Be that taking advantage of workforce development opportunities, educational attainment, or asking for a promotion and greater responsibility at work, what we put into our research and our commitments to training and learning can have positive outcomes and increase our income over time.

Wealth building starts with creating assets—something I had very little guidance on before working in technology startups. For most people of color, and this has certainly been the case for my family, our greatest assets are our homes.

But other forms of leverage across asset classes, like real estate investments, stocks, businesses, and other forms of appreciating opportunities, are becoming much more accessible through the use of technology.

And people of color are even leading the way to help manage these particular asset classes and provide resources to communities that have been traditionally underserved by products and services or lacking financial institutions within our communities.

A Selection of Black and Latinx-Fintech Companies

Cadre

Founder: Ryan Williams

Cadre.com

Allows accredited investors to build their own commercial real estate portfolio at the intersection of private equity and technology.

CapWay

Founder: Sheena Allen

capway.com

CapWay's mobile banking combines social content with technology to better present finance in a way that relates to the next generation.

Freeman Capital

Founder: Calvin Williams

freemancapital.com

Online wealth management and financial planning.

Greenwood

Founders: former Atlanta mayor Andrew Young, rapper–activist Michael Render, and media executive Ryan Glover

bankgreenwood.com

Digital bank under the charter of a larger, traditional bank, targeting Black and Latinx communities.

Guava

Founder: Kelly Ifill

joinguava.com

A digital bank that supports and celebrates Black businesses by providing equitable financial products and connections.

(continued)

(continued)

NovoPayment

Founder: Anabel Perez

novopayment.com

Mobile banking, card solutions, real-time and contactless payments.

SoLo Funds

Founders: Travis Holoway and Rodney Williams

solofunds.com

SoLo funds is a peer-to-peer lending community that allows members to access and supply short-term funds through their app.

Case Study: SoloFunds

Travis Holoway and his college friend Rodney Williams were known as the great success stories in their families. After completing their education and landing high-paying careers, they soon became the go-to loan option for family and friends who reached out often for $20 here and $50 there to put gas in the car, buy groceries, or handle any other necessary expenses while waiting on paychecks.

The two came together in 2017 to launch SoloFunds. The financial technology company provides a peer-to-peer mobile lending platform that facilitates personal loans between borrowers and lenders. Every day, hundreds of thousands of users are borrowing or lending $50 to $1,000 within minutes.

With significant checks and balances on borrower payback success ratings and tips that can be given to the lender for providing the loan, SoloFunds stands in the gap to prevent people from taking out predatory loans via check-cashing or payday lending establishments—an industry where lower-income communities spend upwards of $11 billion per year in fees when interest rates can sometimes exceed 400 percent, further reducing household income and opportunities for upward mobility.

WORD BANK: Cryptocurrency

Cryptocurrency is a form of digital asset based on a network and distributed across computers. The decentralized infrastructure exists outside of the control of governments and traditional banking institutions. It also uses cryptography, making it a secure digital currency that is nearly impossible to counterfeit.

Neobank

A neobank is a direct, online bank that operates exclusively online without physical branches. They offer traditional banking products like savings and checking accounts, budgeting tools, financial education tools, and other services. Many are affiliated with traditional banks for FDIC insurance but are less regulated.

These digital-first and mobile-first banks emerged as recently as 10 years ago, using technology to make the banking experience frictionless and cheaper for users. Pitchbook data reveals that the global customers of these banks will reach 149 million people by 2024.

Fintech

Innovations in this industry aim to use technology to improve the delivery of financial services. The rise in fintech can be seen across digital payment services, peer-to-peer cash lending and payments, and other tools that create efficiencies in access to financial markets and services.

Fractional Stocks

A relatively new way to invest, fractional shares are portions of or small slices of stocks and exchange-traded funds. Instead of paying for a full share of a public-traded company's stock all at once, fractional shares allow you to invest in small increments for as little as $1. Financial institutions from legacy banks like Fidelity, Charles Schwab, and others offer the ability to buy these shares. And rising fintech companies like Stash, Acorns, Robinhood, and others have recently emerged as mobile-first platforms that also let users buy fractional shares.

Action Items

- Plan and host regular money conversations with your family.
- Leverage online tools and resources to improve your financial literacy.
- Research salaries by jobs and industries to set clear expectations when going into negotiations with potential employers.
- Practice negotiating through mock interviews with family, friends, career counselors, and mentors.
- Groups on Facebook, Twitter, Valence, and other social media networking platforms are great places to find technology industry groups of color to learn from and ask questions. You can participate in these groups for free.
- Use your local library, or subscribe to financial newsletters and podcasts to improve your understanding of financial planning, investing, and other wealth-building strategies.

6

Brand or Bust?

THE #ILookLikeAnEngineer hashtag campaign that appeared on Twitter in August 2015 began as an attempt to show the gender diversity in engineering and STEM across the board. More than 75,000 users have leveraged the hashtag since, with an attempt to identify and rebrand what it means to be a professional in the industry.

Social media has added a new level of swag with a variety of self-appointed campaigns to create inclusive representation of science, math, technology, and other professions, both across the country and around the world. Stereotypes be damned, the engineers and tech nerds I follow are diverse, come from a variety of backgrounds, wear Jordans or Patagonia vests, and wear their cultures and hustle proudly.

Despite the visibility of these voices and personalities on social media, the industry itself hasn't always lent itself to visibility at this level—which has required us to get creative about building or succeeding in spaces to show what is possible.

As it stands, the brand of representation hasn't held true in the most significant environments. According to McKinsey's 2020 Women in the Workplace report, for every 100 men who are promoted to the position of manager, only 85 women are promoted, and the gap is even more striking for Black women and Latinas. Only 58 Black women and 71 Latinas were promoted to every 100 men.

As it stands, 41 women are leading Fortune 500 companies—a drop in the bucket. In 2021, Rosalind Brewer from Walgreens Boots Alliance and Thasunda Brown Duckett from TIAA made history as two Black women holding these top positions at the same time.

The Pattern Matching Challenge

Efforts to mitigate and expand access beyond a certain profile are slowly increasing. An analysis of LinkedIn data in 2020 revealed that the number of people globally holding the title of head of diversity more than doubled over the last five years, representing 107 growth.

In 2020 alone, following the murder of George Floyd, over 200 companies made public pledges to revamp their recruitment strategies to increase diverse representation at their companies in 2020 alone. This effort, while not a complete solution to representation within high-tech, high-growth environments, will provide more open doors.

Today, the top 1 percent of high-paying C-suite jobs are still held by white males. The satirical and yet true uniform and background of your typical Silicon Valley tech worker has been maintained: wearing a hoodie, likely graduated from Stanford or Harvard Business School, likely comes from a well-off family, and shares more in common with those who mirror lives or careers like Bill Gates, Mark Zuckerberg, or Elon Musk. The reality is that folks hire people who look like them or come from similar backgrounds or life routes with which they are familiar.

This bias and preference is psychological. Pattern matching or preferences are human nature. We gravitate toward what is familiar, similar, and doesn't cause us to stray too outside our sphere of mental comfort by introducing too much abstract brainpower to consider what is unfamiliar. Of course, our discomfort with the "irregular" trains us to discriminate against any outside information or data, which leads us to harmful outcomes.

When we consider the gaps of representation within industries without people of color or women, there are several factors at play, including issues around investing in these groups, and plain discriminatory practices that keep us out.

Education and training also play a big role in how pattern matching within the technology industry narrows the accessibility for entry. Take for instance the top technology companies, and largest employers, which usually hire from just

Company	Facebook	Amazon	Apple	Microsoft	Google
Schools	University of California–Berkeley	University of Washington	Stanford University	University of Washington	Stanford University
	Stanford University	University of Southern California	University of California–Berkeley	Washington State University	University of California–Berkeley
	Carnegie Mellon University	Arizona State University	University of Texas–Austin	Georgia Institute of Technology	Carnegie Mellon University
	University of Washington	Georgia Institute of Technology	University of Southern California	University of Illinois–Urbana-Champaign	University of California–Los Angeles
	University of California–Los Angeles	University of California–Berkeley	University of California–Los Angeles	Carnegie Mellon University	Massachusetts Institute of Technology

Source: SHL 2020 Aspirational Academics Analysis.

a handful of universities. See the chart on page 123, sourced from an analysis by SHL of over 800,000 LinkedIn profiles of employees across a variety of tech companies.

This analysis can provide a few options for our understanding of how feeder schools and networks play a role in understanding how the industry works and thinks. Closed networks are often about matching the profile or branding oneself to assimilate and conform to the mold.

Increasing college costs and sharpening selectivity at top colleges doesn't mean that outliers can't exist—they do signal, however, that branding ourselves still takes a required and measured approach to how we enter the spaces in which we intend to find our successes. These can often be exceptions and not the rule.

What matters, when you don't necessarily have access, is intentionally designing our pathways.

The Story You're Looking to Tell

I wasn't strategic in my college selection process the first time around. The thought in my family and what was pushed in my school community was that college, of any sort, was going to be a guaranteed foot in the door to opportunity. I had no regard for how to select the right school, which programs I would need to have access to, or which employers were connected to most universities and would offer me an academic experience that was on par with industry needs.

For my graduate program, I was a bit more calculated. I attended one of the top journalism programs in the country because it offered a few things I needed at the time to make myself competitive in the job market: in-demand skills.

Studying data and journalism was my resolve to improve my analytical skills and, of course, pursue a path of entrepreneurship in an industry where my program was at the school that most executives and media leaders had attended. Graduate school was an expensive endeavor that has surely paid its weight in opportunities but was a tremendous investment that I had not prepared for financially.

But I was in charge of shaping a narrative that would lead me into the fields and rooms I needed to access that previously weren't open. I needed to follow and tell a story as I stacked my career experience, unsure if entrepreneurship would work out; I knew that I needed to appear competitive no matter what happened.

Learning how to tell my story through my career endeavors was a lesson in personal branding I didn't become equipped with until my mid-20s.

After getting laid off from my first job out of college, and facing a harsh economy as a result of the recession, getting my footing meant reimagining myself and my work, and finding pathways into industries that were growing and not yet clearly defined.

My college friend, Enovia, and I attended the Fashion Institute of Technology together, landed internships, and even our dream jobs, but still didn't have the development skills or networks to easily find an inroad into work. We freelanced, hustled, did odd jobs, built websites, and tried our hands at entrepreneurship, hitting roadblocks and being late on the rent most months.

I had a successful blog, but quickly became disenchanted with just a little bit of cash and a few beauty products each month. Working for small brands meant all-hands with little guidance, and I knew that I needed a bit more structure and refinement to move beyond where I'd been able to reach in the bits of a career I had managed to establish.

I knew I was missing the critical professional development and coaching that came with working full time for large companies. So I applied for a public policy fellowship that matched talented young professionals with executive coaches. I figured changing the country would include working within government to help address issues of climate, education, and entrepreneurship.

The program would be based in Bridgeport, Connecticut. I'd done plenty of internships, but a fellowship felt prestigious, and it came with a decent salary. I'd never been to the state of Connecticut, and at the time, I had locs and multicolored hair, half of my head was shaved, and I had very little conservative clothing for a government environment built in the color of blues and grays.

I packed up my bed and mattress, a few suitcases, and what little kitchen items I had into a small U-Haul truck and made the trip from New Jersey, another place I shared with Enovia, and set off to my new apartment, which was a 600-square-foot gem housed in a former bank building turned into high-rise apartments.

This was a turning point for me. Despite its conservative climate, working for the mayor's office in Bridgeport made me mentally tough. I learned the fine art of community engagement, navigating challenging political climates, leading in a position where I was not necessarily in charge, and managing to learn how to develop executive presence.

My executive coach, Anne, helped me move from nervous young energy to seeing myself as a leader and taking up space.

One of the assignments required by the fellowship program was to have an understanding of our leadership style, as well as how we wanted to shape our list of filtering criteria. What were we looking for? What did we need above just a name?

I remember Anne showing me how to run an effective meeting. We sat in an empty conference room in the mayor's office. She had me set up the empty boardroom and pretend that I was running a meeting. I sat at the head of the table as Anne walked me through proper facilitation methods. Prior to doing this exercise with Anne, I was a nervous wreck in meetings. The work of government was so remarkably unfamiliar to me that I was afraid I would say the wrong thing. I didn't want my nervous energy to translate into not being taken seriously in my role, so I had to practice sharpening my skills until I felt comfortable enough to call, run, and facilitate meetings on my own.

But my most important lesson during that time was how to create a framework for developing my personal brand, empowered by what my internship director Meghan called my filtering criteria, to make decisive choices about where I wanted to end up, both personally and professionally.

Meghan came to my office one afternoon, hassling me about what I would do after the fellowship ended. I had a few local offers on the table but wasn't sure whom to say yes to. I just knew that going without an income was not an option. Student loans still had to be paid, and after making it through a recession with inconsistent income, I wasn't ready to go back to the struggle.

I felt like I had to make a choice that I wasn't 100 percent convinced would put me in a position to get to the next level in my professional career. And after spending a year in a city without many friends, a network that was only accessible because of whom I worked for, I knew that remaining in the city wouldn't offer me the best shot at developing a sustainable social life. I needed to be in a bigger city, and out of local politics.

"The problem is that you will never be lacking in opportunities," Meghan said. "You'll now have to decide which opportunities are going to be important by adjusting them against your filtering criteria."

It was one of the few moments in my life that I felt a bit more in control of my next steps. I had to let go of the fear that everything was going to come crashing down. Still dealing with a bit of PTSD from my layoff during the recession, and finally feeling like I was getting back on my feet, that bit of advice would shape much of my choice of professional and personal paths over the next eight years.

It's a framework I still use today to evaluate opportunities that come into my orbit, and share them with my mentees as they navigate their careers.

In a sea of what was a desperate time, that experience taught me that I still have a choice and that I can use my time much more wisely by offering myself the choice to filter what would be for me and what wouldn't.

As I wrapped up my fellowship, it was clear that the environment I needed to be in would be one of helping to shape the world through technology. I began charting out my next series of experiences and the kind of city I would need to live in for that to be a reality. I wanted to be in an environment where more people of color were in positions of power. I had grown tired of being one of very few in a room. I wanted to be in a city that was growing, diverse, had principles of sustainability, good transportation systems (I didn't own a car), an affordable cost of living, and access to a variety of potential employers.

Following that meeting with Meghan, I created a list of attributes that would define my filtering criteria for both the city I wanted to live in and the type of job I would want to have:

- I want to work on something that is changing society for the better and moving us forward.
- I want to work on a team of smart and talented people that I can learn from.
- I don't want to be the "only" at the table. I want to work and live in a city that values diversity.
- I have to join a technology company. I want to work in a startup where my contributions will make a difference and I'll be able to directly influence the business.
- I want to work for a company that has clear pathways for growth and upward mobility.
- I want to be able to travel the world with my next company and earn opportunities to work abroad with team members that are different from me.

Tired of New York, and not interested in staying in Connecticut, I set my sights on the city of Charlotte, North Carolina.

Aunt Benita, another close family friend who taught me the ropes of entrepreneurship in my early years, had moved to the city from Seattle just a few months earlier and opened her home to me. I'd be back on someone's sofa, but at least I'd feel in charge of where I was headed and why.

As my lease ended, I sold my things on Craigslist, including a $50 velvet Victorian sofa I flipped for $300, packed up a rented minivan, and made the drive to Charlotte with my childhood friend Demyla, who flew in from Seattle to help me start my new life.

I had no job, no real plan, and only three months before the little bit of cash I had saved up would run out.

Career Development Books Written by Women and People of Color

Build Your Dream Network by J. Kelly Hoey

Future Proofed by Natalia Peart, PhD

Let Them See You by Porter Braswell

Next Move Best Move by Kimberly Cummings

Strategize to Win by Carla A. Harris

Talking to Strangers by Malcolm Gladwell

Three months later, I'd landed at Uber, helping to run marketing campaigns and partnerships for the Charlotte market.

My subsequent stacking of social capital included networking across the industry, setting up coffee meetings with key players in tech and entrepreneurship, building legit friendships, and participating in the community as often as I could to keep abreast of what was happening in the city and also position myself for any future opportunities that could come as a result of being plugged-in and visible.

At the top of being intentional about my experience, particularly in a new city where I had no family and had to build my reputation from the ground up, I always questioned my movements with: Where did I need to volunteer in order to build community and feel better connected with the learnings and understanding of where I could best use my talent? Which boards did I want to be part of where I could offer my network and talents?

That strategy paid dividends. I was able to transition from Uber to several consulting jobs with local companies, eventually landing an opportunity as a contractor with Google Fiber, and when I launched BLKTECHCLT, it was easy to rally support and get access to grants.

I was in a space of thriving and stacking up a resume with high-profile opportunities.

At some point, realizing the future was data and that those skills needed to be improved, I looked around, realizing that my sole marketing degree wasn't going to be enough to get me to move vertically through any top-tier company, and although I was slowly building The Plug, it was still a grind. So I decided I needed another subset of education that would allow me to demonstrate my prowess.

I looked around at local analytics certificate programs, things I could complete within a six- to nine-month time frame that required minimal investment of both time and resources. In my pursuit, most were tailored to banking, an industry I knew I wouldn't survive in. An online search showed me a program at Columbia that could be completed in 10 months, award me a master's, and help me sharpen my journalism skills while also deepening my computational skills. The hybrid program, if I could get in, seemed like a good buy—a master's degree, a top-tier university, the ability to earn credentials that could still transfer over to technology as marketing teams became the leading arbiters of analytics, and only 10 months to get it done.

After getting my acceptance letter, I packed up my Charlotte apartment, rented a room at Enovia's mom's home in Harlem, and started my program with a clear intent: make myself marketable and competitive for both my business and the job market.

Unlike undergrad, I knew exactly what I was planning to get out of the program. I knew which programs were feeders, which networks recruited, and which spaces also offered access to the top minds. At school, I went to lectures and networking events next door at the Data Science Institute and the business school, meeting other students, speaking to faculty, and attending conferences and lectures when my schedule would allow.

My decisions were guided by a few principal questions: What kind of money did I want to earn? Was it an additional $20,000, $50,000, or $100,000? What were my intended outcomes? Which professionals in which careers were examples of spaces I'd like to occupy upon reaching my goals? Which jobs had just been invented? When I was graduating from undergrad, social media manager titles had just become a thing. What materials could I be reading to make it all so? I had to apply a layer of scrutiny to my resume, my skills, my talents, and assess what was missing so that I could continue to make myself competitive.

Some of these activities helped me connect with recruiters at various tech companies and foundations—private invitations to fancy events where recruiters gave you their direct email and followed up profusely.

Partnerships and introductions to executives and professionals were made easier when they immediately acknowledged that I was completing my education at the same school their sibling, parents, spouse, or they themselves had gone to. Did it automatically help me land the opportunity? Of course not. My ability to sell and market myself did that. But it often eased the discussion or at least got me in the door.

Building up a personal brand for myself was holistic. I made myself and my work visible online, publicizing what panel I had spoken on, what article I had published, where I was working, which articles I was reading, or anything that would allow me to remind my network about the breakthroughs and accomplishments I was experiencing in my career.

Certainly, I didn't always get it right, but I leveraged the mental models, the utility of the internet, and the emerging platforms, making it easier for me to access the professional spaces I wanted to be part of, and a framework for making decisions so that I could feel in control over my professional experience and eventual path into entrepreneurship.

Building Your Professional Brand Online

Determine what you'd like the world to know about you and your skills.

Standing out from the crowd as a candidate means letting your digital footprint speak for you before you ever land an interview or speak with a recruiter about your qualifications. Developing your personal brand and building lasting connections means being authentic and transparent about your skills, capabilities, work experience, and career aspirations.

Decide who your audience is.

Are you looking to land at a small and scrappy startup where you're more likely to have lots of face time with the

(continued)

(continued)

leadership team? Do you want to work for a big company that has a few decades of skin in the game and you're looking to join a team with clearly defined roles and expectations? Learn the language of each, and begin tailoring your personal brand to that industry.

Leverage existing platforms to build your profile.

Free platforms like LinkedIn provide easy-to-set-up profiles that instantly connect you with thousands of professionals. You can build a portfolio. List what you accomplished at past jobs. Showcase your work. Comment and engage with other professionals who share updates and respectfully reach out to people in your network to further develop connections. You can also search and apply for open jobs.

Other free platforms you can use to create your own domain name and customize your personal website experience include Wix.com, SquareSpace.com, Wordpress .com, and many others.

Develop your portfolio and professional content.

Turn any meaningful projects and work products that you feel proud of and are relevant to your industry into a sales page for your skillsets. Add any relevant articles you were featured in or write them yourself, sharing your opinions, learnings from a recent conference, class projects you're working through, experiences and lessons learned, and so on. Use editing tools like Canva to create graphics and Grammarly to help with editing your writing and demonstrate your communications skills.

Know what you're looking for.

If you're in the market for a new job opportunity or switching careers and just looking for help navigating the new environment, be clear about your intent. Practice and rehearse your "elevator pitch" so that you're asking for specific support aligned with your goals.

Make it easy for recruiters and employers to contact you.

If you choose to host your resume and portfolio on your own website, make sure there is a contact form, email address, or link to your LinkedIn page to make it easy to send potential employers your way.

Maintain your privacy but showcase your talents.

Remember that this is a professional profile designed to showcase your skills and capabilities and help you to brand yourself as a serious professional in the field. Add your personality and authenticity, but also be mindful of keeping things professional and protecting your privacy. Never share personal information like your direct phone number, home address, your children's schools, or any information you wouldn't want to be published on the internet.

Today, there are plenty of coaches who can help us navigate our careers, negotiation tactics, and everything. Price points can range from private membership clubs where you learn in a virtual group setting or can work one-on-one at a higher price. The investment will pay dividends when you have the tools to advocate for yourself and know how to best package your work and experience and position yourself for a job of the future.

If you are looking to transition into tech careers or work for technology companies, positioning yourself for these roles also includes creating evidence of your work and your knowledge. This can look like getting support with building an online profile and portfolio be it on LinkedIn, your own website, or any other platform that helps you to create a digital footprint that you have control over.

Employers, colleagues, and recruiters are going first to the internet to perform a digital background check of your name and social media accounts. This trend definitely increased as social media took over in the early 2010s, making what we do in our personal lives on the internet accessible publicly. Instantly, we were all building brands and versions of ourselves that could be easily excavated for poor behavior from employers, family members, and networks.

Breaking into and Building Startups with No Brand

Clarence Bethea doesn't care for titles or any particular pedigree. He's said as much publicly, tweeting through a string of expectations he's vocally acknowledged where he doesn't fit the profile or any of the tags and keywords typically associated with being a tech founder. He didn't attend a prestigious university, join a popular fraternity, or decorate himself with any of the top consulting firms that might have provided inroads into environments where resumes of similar nature are almost a rite of passage.

Instead, Bethea built Upsie from the ground up, starting the company from his St. Paul, Minnesota, home in 2013.

Upsie's platform provides warranty coverage designed to make purchasing and storing these warranties easy and affordable. Instead of purchasing a warranty from a retailer or manufacturer, users can compare prices and terms, purchase on the platform, receive warnings when warranties are set to expire, and protect their products and devices at affordable rates.

I met Clarence during my 2016 Virginia press tour with venture capital ecosystem organization Village Capital when Upsie was still getting off the ground and had raised at least $1.5 million in seed capital.

He'd been proving the industry wrong—you didn't need a certain profile to play the game, you just had to win, stay diligent, leverage the resources around you, build a strong network by proving your business model and work ethic. A proud contrarian, Bethea has still managed to see success by leveraging the tools around him and today boasts having raised over $20 million for his company and employs over 20 employees.

Social Capital or Bust?

WORD BANK: Social Capital

noun: Sociology.

The interpersonal relationships, institutions, and other social assets of a society or group that can be used to gain an advantage.

Source: Dictionary.com.

The old adage "It's not what you know, it's whom you know" holds a great deal of weight. Connections, institutions, organizations, associations, and other forms of cultivated environments, whether we like them or not, play heavily into how we access various forms of mobility, socially and economically, based on our connectivity to these networks.

Social capital has bred inequality in many forms across public policies in education, housing, food and transportation access, banking, and the criminal justice system. Social exclusion looks like not having working transportation systems that can bring you from your neighborhood to areas of high-employment opportunities. Concentrated housing and affordable neighborhoods redlined and concentrated creates the potential for not having access to a diversity of neighbors of various income or career levels.

To change the dynamics, efforts to improve mobility have been the topic of research over the past two decades.

Research shows us that most people of color lack social capital—the kind that will enable us to make more money or get access to top jobs the deeper and more prestigious our networks.

A Brookings Institution study of interpersonal networks and economic mobility of residents in Racine, Wisconsin, San Francisco, California, and Washington, DC found that white men have the most racially homogeneous networks. Black men have the least robust social networks. And those living in cities with lower economic mobility have the most racially homogeneous social networks.

The cities were chosen for their various degrees of economic, racial, and gender diversity, with San Francisco as a high mobility city, Washington, DC a moderate economic mobility city, and Racine ranking lower on mobility.

The researchers found that San Francisco, as a city, has the least racially homogeneous social networks, but when it comes to white people, San Francisco sticks out as having the most homogeneity compared to other racial groups. The sample study provides a lens into how staying committed within the confines of just one group limits our potential for access to new information, experiences, and networks, especially if you're earning on the lower end of the pay spectrum.

The digital landscape has offered closer connection points that were previously unavailable to those not in proximity to institutions and people and job opportunities of note. From platforms like Valence, EnrichHer, AfroTech, Latinas in Tech, Athena Alliance, and others, these digital environments offer mentorship matching, career development workshops, networking, and more. Platforms like Twitter, Instagram, LinkedIn, and others, if used correctly, can also put you in touch with job opportunities and other networks.

How you show up online matters. So using these platforms strategically, perhaps to add your personal website and portfolio, engage in conversations about your industry to stand out and appear knowledgeable.

Action Items

Stay Ready So You Don't Have to Get Ready

- **Interviewing.** Interviewing is both art and science. Whether you're looking for your next opportunity or just want to refresh your skills, asking for informational interviews as you're researching careers or learning about different and emerging trends in an industry, practice your interview techniques with professionals in your industry.
- **Career development.** I used resources like Mindtools .com to help me gain access to frameworks for career building, leadership, and more. Other programs from career

7

Owning the Moment

WHAT IF THE future of work isn't just about getting a job but is also about creating one?

Small business creation is a key driver in securing the jobs of tomorrow. In the United States, small businesses account for almost 50 percent of the country's private workforce. Before the recession, small businesses alone added 1.8 million new jobs to the economy.

Having muddled through a pandemic and an economic recession over the past decade, entrepreneurship growth rates across states have waned, comparing a decline of 17.1 percentage points between 2019 and 2020 with just 6.9 percent of businesses created between 2008 and 2009, according to a Kauffman Foundation study.

The types of businesses that have emerged have changed drastically, thanks to the internet. No longer do you need large amounts of capital to put your idea into the marketplace. Thanks to online platforms, instant access to customers, and the growth of several social media tools, creating, launching, marketing, and growing a business has never been easier.

While in undergrad, I launched an online newswire service business with a friend. The business wasn't anything to write home about, and it certainly didn't land me in the pages of *Forbes*, but it was an easy setup that only required a $10 domain name, a quick blog design I paid about $300 for a classmate who was studying graphic design to create, and a free email marketing platform I could use to reach prospective customers.

The company was called LadyPR, and we helped companies looking to reach women by targeting their press releases to our list of editors and journalists at top media companies. After a few internship stints with boutique public relations firms, I had built up a hefty list of contacts of media players that I was able to turn into an asset for my business. I advertised the resource across social media and through a weekly email newsletter and regularly attending events hosted by women's business associations and groups, where I pitched our service offering.

I charged clients anywhere from $100 to $300 to send a press release to our contacts. The site wasn't fancy. I paid a classmate from the design program $150 for a basic design and built a contact form where customers could upload their resumes, select the types of publications they wanted their press releases to be shared with, and hit "submit." I'd then create a segment within our email service provider, and schedule the press release.

That small business paid the rent for about a year. If I had taken the time to automate it, it could have grown, but I grew tired and disenchanted with the concept and was ready to try something new. Not to mention that, during that time, we were headed into a recession, where most PR and marketing teams were being cut or spending was reduced significantly, and most of our business began to dry up.

The point is, I was able to quite easily, for less than $500, launch a business, start working with clients, and quickly start earning revenue.

A New Class of Entrepreneurs

When I began writing for major publishers, I was determined to write about the everyday Black and brown entrepreneurs I was meeting in my work, at conferences, and finding online who were defining an aspect of the technology industry with their apps and ideas that weren't seeing a great deal of coverage in mainstream news.

Recognition of innovation hubs outside of Silicon Valley and New York was hard-won, as the narratives of hot new tech startups in these markets dominated the narrative of where innovation comes from.

For those paying attention, rising groups and movements enabled by the internet, social media, and increased travel and online networking began fueling greater opportunities for Black and brown founders. And the idea of access to more networks was being challenged, as new data was revealing how discriminatory capital and networks were against geographies and race.

Research studies were fueling the idea that there was a disparity in funding and opportunities for entrepreneurs of color. Early reports of this disparity noted that the majority of all venture capital, to the tune of 97 percent, was invested in white and male teams—with just under 2 percent invested in founders of color.

Those dollars also skipped over the environments where the vast majority of people of color live, like the Midwest, South, and Southeast. Instead, those dollars were concentrated in places like my hometown of Seattle and in California, New York, Washington, DC, Massachusetts, and Connecticut.

I remember connecting with Rodney Sampson for the first time following our first meeting at the SXSW tech conference in 2016. Rodney and several others were doing the work of facilitating relationships between new angel investors who made their money in government contracts, construction, and other fields and new up-and-coming technology entrepreneurs.

Rodney, who had built and sold a streaming platform for churches to broadcast sermons on his platform, Streaming Faith, was helping to build out accelerators and co-working spaces in the city of Atlanta. His network of high-net-worth entrepreneurs and colleagues became the vehicle he used to teach them about the benefits of investing in technology enterprises.

This was a new field of study for those who were used to seeing, touching, and feeling an investment like a restaurant, bar, barbershop, laundromat, and other forms of brick-and-mortar stores that many of us have seen and understand within our neighborhoods. But software? That was another beast with a learning curve for understanding how to invest in and the opportunity for success within a market that felt invisible.

I wrote a story for *Fast Company* in 2013 documenting the journey and the rise of Black venture capitalists shaping new opportunities for Black entrepreneurs and other entrepreneurs of color. As money began to shift, Black and brown people, who felt the disparity long before the studies hit the headlines, were working to help fill in the gaps.

And as the demand for greater resources and research on the deficits continued to come to light, Black investors, and those aspiring to be investors, began stepping up to help talented entrepreneurs get the support they needed.

The earliest venture fund led by Black fund managers could have been Syncom in 1977. They were one of the first investors in Black Entertainment Television, led by Bob and Sheila Johnson.

Recognizing the growth in opportunity, as Black and Latinx entrepreneurs began to ask for their piece of the venture capital support, so did the rise of Black fund managers launching opportunities to create routes to capital for those who traditionally didn't have networks to rely on within the tech industry. Today, more than 80 venture firms led by Black fund managers exist today. And those firms boast highly diverse teams and companies they've invested in.

Renewable Energy and Clean Technologies

Considering the rapid challenges our atmosphere and climates are facing on a warming planet, companies have invested in pushing us off of fossil fuels, reducing waste, carbon dioxide emissions, and other wasteful behaviors that are contributing to massive things like droughts, deforestation, and wildfires; innovation is stepping up to the plate in an effort to reverse this trend and lessen our reliance on fossil fuels.

While the clean technology and renewable energy sectors are not new (the earliest solar panel technologies were built by Bell Labs in the 1950s), the market is rapidly increasing due to demand, greater sophistication, and the race to address global climate and natural disaster instances around the globe.

Cheat Code

- Software developers are the number-one tech job of the future, with expected job growth of 22 percent between 2019 and 2029, adding an additional 316,00 jobs to the market.
- Jobs in information security will be the second most in-demand in the coming years, with expected job growth of 31 percent between 2019 and 2029. Information security positions will require employees with firewall administration and coding.
- Business analysts make approximately $88,000 per year and have educational backgrounds in business and computer technology. Positions as business analysts will be the third most popular in the near future, with expected job growth of 11 percent between 2019 and 2029, adding an additional 93,800 jobs to the market.

The Top Tech Jobs Driving the Future

Now that we're clear on what the research is saying will be the most likely jobs at risk for over 25 percent of the American workforce, we can turn our attention to what researchers and the data are saying will be the technologies of the future—and those that are still to come. We can look across the board at the skills that will be necessary to fulfill the demand of people building products, services, and businesses in these spaces.

Understanding which jobs and technologies are driving the future of work helps us better navigate our choices and educational paths, giving us insight into which programs and opportunities will lead us into the fields of work that are most promising and provide long-term stability against potential automation.

The next subsections outline the top jobs defining the future of work, the expected salary ranges, an understanding of what the role entails, which kind of employers are typically hiring for these sorts of roles, and typical prerequisites for entering the field.

Of course, there are a plethora of different entry points and technologies, and emerging trends that will continue to drive and transform the future. For instance, platforms like Facebook and Twitter didn't exist 20 years ago. As new technology companies are created, so are jobs that will require a mix of trained skills and emerging adaptability.

15 In-Demand Tech Jobs

The following jobs defining the U.S. technology industry are based on an analysis of current employment data, projected job openings, anticipated job growth, and employer outlooks on labor needs through 2029.

For every job identified, you'll get an understanding of what the job entails and the education and skill requirements needed for the position.

PRO TIP

How can you stay on industry trends and opportunities as the workforce changes rapidly? Follow the top employers in the spaces that you are interested in, watch labor statistics reports, and follow news publications that are making this information available to the public.

Software Developer   As the primary tech job of the future, the Bureau of Labor Statistics anticipates job growth to increase by 22 percent for this profession through 2029, adding over 300,000 jobs to the market. Developers write and program computer programs and applications for a majority of the tools we use today on our smartphones and online.

2020 median salary: $110,000

- Prerequisites:
  - Bachelor's degree in computer science, computer programming, or software engineering

- Associated tech skills:
  - Certifications in Microsoft, Amazon Software Services, Cloudera, Oracle
  - ASP.NET
  - JavaScript
  - Java
  - C#
  - Python

Information Security   Information security analysts are the ninjas of the tech world, responsible for preventing, responding to, and monitoring cyberattacks and data breaches.
2020 median salary: $100,000

- Prerequisites:
  - Bachelor's degree in computer science, information assurance, programming
  - Master of Business Administration (MBA) in information systems
  - Certified Information Systems Security Professional (CISSP)
  - Certified Ethical Hacker (CEH)
  - CompTIA Security+

- Associated tech skills:
  - Reverse engineering
  - Python
  - Shell
  - Java
  - C#
  - Application design
  - Firewall administration
  - SEIM tools

Business Analysts   Business analysts work with and compute data within their respective industries and at their companies to help companies determine their performance and help to make key strategic business decisions.
Median salary: $85,000

- Prerequisites:
  - Bachelor's degree in business, computer and information technology, mathematics
  - Master of Business Administration (MBA)
  - Certified Management Consultant (CMC)

- Associated tech skills:
  - Data analysis
  - SQL
  - Data visualization
  - Statistical analysis software
  - Survey and query software
  - Business intelligence and reporting software
  - Data mining
  - Database design

Cybersecurity   From analyst to management positions, these professionals work to prevent cyberattacks and create digital architecture to keep out intruders. They also do forensics to understand how attacks happened to prevent future hacks.
Median salary: $102,000

- Prerequisites:
  - Bachelor's degree in cybersecurity, computer programming, computer and information sciences
  - Cisco Certified Network Associate (CCNA, routing, and switching)
  - Certified Information Security Manager (CISM)
  - CompTIA Security+ Base-Level Certification
  - Systems Administration and Network Security Certifications (SANS)

- ○ Certified Ethical Hacker (CEH)
- ○ Offensive Security Certified Professional (OSCP)
- ○ Certified Information Security Auditor (CISA)
- ○ CIAC Certified Incident Handler (GCIH)
- ○ Certified Information Systems Security Professional (CISSP)
- ○ Information Systems Security Architecture Professional (CISSP-ISSAP)
- ○ Information Systems Security Engineering Professional (CISSP-ISSEP)
- ○ Information Systems Security Management Professional (CISSP-ISSMP)

- ■ Associated tech skills:
  - ○ Operating systems
  - ○ Virtualization software
  - ○ Programming and software development
  - ○ Software analytics
  - ○ Programming languages (Java, C#, PHP, Python, Perl, Shell)

IT Manager/Director   In this role, managers and directors of IT departments are responsible for guiding the technology strategies and goals of a business, running cost analyses, scheduling maintenance, selecting technology, and the ongoing support of overall infrastructure.

Median salary: $150,000

- ■ Prerequisites:
  - ○ Bachelor's degree in computer and information technology, engineering technologies, management information

systems (MIS), software development, computer programming
- o Master of Business Administration (MBA)
- o Project Management Professional (PMP)
- o PMI Agile Certified Practitioner (PMI-ACP)
- o CompTIA Project+
- o Certified ScrumMaster (CSM)
- o Product Management from Pragmatic Institute
- o ITIL
- o Certified in the Governance of Enterprise IT (CGEIT)

- ■ Associated tech skills:
  - o Information technology
  - o Vendor management
  - o Computer science
  - o ERP systems
  - o Disaster recovery planning
  - o Virtualization
  - o SQL
  - o Help desk support
  - o Deployment

Computer Systems Analyst   This person is responsible for making recommendations on which computer systems an organization should use and why. They might also construct ways to use existing technology in tandem with other technologies, and train employees overall on how to use the software.
Median salary: $93,730

- ■ Prerequisites:
  - o Bachelor's degree in computer and information technology, mathematics, Management Information Systems

- o Master of Business Administration (MBA) in information technology
- o Master of Science (MS) in cybersecurity
- o Master of Science (MS) in software development
- o CompTIA A+ Certification
- o CompTIA Security+
- o CompTIA CySA+
- o CASP+

- ■ Associated tech skills:
  - o Database design
  - o Management principles
  - o Systems architecture
  - o Systems analysis
  - o Hardware configuration
  - o Training

Help Desk/Computer Support   Falling in the category of customer service, employees in these positions support software users with feedback, advice, and troubleshooting technical assistance. Many of these jobs are remote, requiring a strong internet connection, a computer, and phone device.

Median salary: $55,000

- ■ Prerequisites:
  - o Computer-related coursework or experience
  - o Bachelor's degree in liberal arts, computer programming
  - o CompTIA A+
  - o CompTIA Network+
  - o CompTIA Security+
  - o MCSDA: Windows
  - o MCSE: Desktop Infrastructure

- Associated tech skills:
  - Technology installation
  - Customer service
  - Remote technical support
  - File backup and restoration
  - Operating system maintenance
  - Problem solving

DevOps Engineer   Working at the intersection of software development and engineering, these professionals make sure that technology is working efficiently in development, testing, and production. They work collaboratively across departments.

- Prerequisites:
  - Bachelor's degree in cloud computing, enterprise networks, computer programming
  - Master of Business Administration (MBA) in technology management
  - CompTIA Linux+
  - Microsoft Certified Solutions Associate (MCSA)
  - Certificate of Cloud Security Knowledge (CCSK)

- Associated tech skills:
  - Infrastructure management
  - Security oversight
  - Automation management
  - Software Development Life Cycle (SDLC)
  - Agile development
  - Continuous integration (CI)
  - Continuous delivery (CD)
  - Source/version control
  - Orchestration

- ○ Container management
- ○ Cloud architecture
- ○ Programming knowledge (Java, Python, C#, Ruby, G, PHP, JavaScript)

Data Scientist   Comprising a combination of statistics and mathematical analyses to compile and model data for business, professionals in this role can work across business operations to technical roles.

- ■ Prerequisites:
  - ○ Bachelor's degree in computer science, data science, business analytics
  - ○ Master's degree or PhD in data science, statistics
  - ○ Certified Analytics Professional (CAP)
  - ○ SAS Certified Predictive Modeler using SAS Enterprise Miner 14
  - ○ Cloudera Certified Associate (CCA) Data Analyst
  - ○ Cloudera Certified Professional (CCP) Data Engineer
  - ○ Data Science Council of America (DASCA) Senior Data Scientist (SDS)
  - ○ Data Science Council of America (DASCA) Principal Data Scientist (PDS)
  - ○ Dell EMC Data Science Track (EMCDS)
  - ○ Google Professional Data Engineer Certification
  - ○ IBM Data Science Professional Certificate
  - ○ Microsoft Certified: Azure AI Fundamentals
  - ○ Microsoft Certified: Azure Data Scientist Associate
  - ○ Open Certified Data Scientist (Open CDS)
  - ○ SAS Certified AI & Machine Learning Professional
  - ○ SAS Certified Big Data Professional
  - ○ SAS Certified Data Scientist
  - ○ Tensorflow Developer Certificate

- Associated tech skills:
  - Programming
  - Machine learning
  - Data visualization and reporting
  - Risk analysis
  - Statistical analysis
  - Software engineering
  - Data mining, cleaning, and munging
  - Big data platforms
  - Cloud tools
  - Data warehousing and structures

Cloud/Computer Network Architect   Computer network architects implement communication networks for businesses and customers using the cloud to run their companies. They assist with the upkeep of these systems.

- Prerequisites:
  - Bachelor's degree in computer science, information systems, engineering
  - Master of Business Administration (MBA) in information systems
  - Salesforce Certified Technical Architect (CTA)
  - ITIL Master
  - Red Hat Certified Architect (RHCA)
  - The Open Group TOGAF 9
  - Zachman Certified—Enterprise Architect
  - VMware VCP6-NV
  - Cisco Network Programmability Design and Implementation Specialist (NPDESI)
  - PMI Project Management Professional (PMP)
  - Certified Information Systems Security Professional (CISSP)

- Associated tech skills:
  - Computer operating
  - Computer security
  - Wireless systems
  - Designing data network systems
  - Network repair and maintenance
  - Computer networking
  - Communication systems
  - Project management

Database Administrator   Database administrators (DBAs) analyze the efficiencies of a company's database infrastructure and prevent unauthorized use of systems. They oversee the testing and support queries when new systems are adopted and installed.

Median salary: $98,000

- Prerequisites:
  - Bachelor's degree in management information systems (MIS), computer science
  - Oracle DB Certified Associate
  - Oracle DB Certified Professional
  - Microsoft SQL Server: MCSE and MCDBA
  - IBM Analytics Certification
  - MySQL Database Developer
  - MySQL Database Administrator
  - MongoDB Certified DBA
  - MongoDB Certified Developer
  - Cassandra Certified Administrator
  - Cassandra Certified Architect
  - Cassandra Certified Developer

- Associated tech skills:
  - Database languages
  - SQL
  - Database installation
  - Database configuration
  - Data security
  - User creation and maintenance
  - Database backups and recovery
  - Database performance tuning and optimization
  - Data transformation and loading
  - Reporting and querying

Mobile Application Developer   Application developers write and design for mobile devices like cell phones and tablets, constructing apps for both iOs and Androids.
Median salary: $100,000

- Prerequisites:
  - Bachelor's degree in software engineering, computer science, mobile development
  - Associate Android Developer
  - GIAC Mobile Device Security Analyst (GIAC)
  - MCSD: App Builder
  - MTA Developer
  - Salesforce Certified Platform App Builder

- Associated tech skills:
  - Android—Java and Kotlin, Eclipse
  - iOS (Apple)—Objective-C and Swift, Xcode
  - BlackBerry—Java, Eclipse
  - Symbian—C++
  - Windows Mobile—C#, Microsoft Visual Studio

Web Developer   These professionals often design, develop, and maintain websites across the internet and mobile web.
  Median salary: $77,000

- Prerequisites:
  - Computer-related coursework and experience
  - Bachelor's degree in computer science, computer programming
  - Red Hat Certification
  - Oracle Certified Professional
  - Professional Scrum Developer Certification
  - GIAC Certified Web Application Defender (GWEB)
  - Adobe Certified Expert (ACE)

- Associated tech skills:
  - HTML/CSS
  - Responsive design
  - JavaScript
  - Testing and debugging
  - Back-end basics
  - Search engine optimization
  - Hosting
  - Libraries and frameworks
  - Debugging
  - GIT (code versioning)

Programmer Coding developers and programmers are responsible for writing applications, systems, and networks for any and all technical products that a business and/or consumer may use on a tech-related product. Depending on a business's needs, a coding developer may need various skill sets and have to know particular coding languages, including but not limited to Python, C#, Java, or PHP.

Median salary: $89,000

- Prerequisites:
  - Bachelor's degree in computer science, computer programming, information systems
  - Google Certified Professional Cloud Architect
  - C and C++ Certifications
  - Certified Secure Software Lifecycle Professional (CSSLP)
  - Puppet Labs Puppet Developer
  - Cloudera Certifications
  - Oracle Application Express Developer Certified Expert
  - Certified ScrumMaster
  - CompTIA Security+
  - ITIL
  - AWS Certified Developer
  - Microsoft Certified Solutions Developer (MCSD)

- Associated tech skills:
  - Coding languages (Java, PHP, Python, C#, etc.)
  - Database management
  - Programming
  - HTML/CSS
  - JavaScript
  - MySQL
  - Integrated development environments

Data Analyst Data analysts carry out a role similar to that of data scientists in that they are responsible for compiling

data that doesn't fall into a company's system database and then using that information to help guide business decisions. Data analysts will sometimes write programs that help mine data, which scientists then formulate for strategic purposes.
Median salary: $70,000

- Prerequisites:
  - Bachelor's degree in mathematics, economics, computer science
  - Associate Certified Analytics Professional (aCAP)
  - Certification of Professional Achievement in Data Sciences
  - Certified Analytics Professional
  - Cloudera Certified Associate (CCA) Data Analyst
  - EMC Proven Professional Data Scientist Associate (EMCDSA)
  - IBM Data Science Professional Certificate
  - Microsoft Certified Azure Data Scientist Associate
  - Microsoft Certified Data Analyst Associate
  - Open Certified Data Scientist
  - SAS Certified Advanced Analytics Professional Using SAS 9
  - SAS Certified Big Data Professional Using SAS 9

- Associated tech skills:
  - SQL
  - Microsoft Excel/spreadsheets
  - R or Python-Statistical Programming
  - Data visualization
  - Machine learning
  - Data warehousing

Action Items

- Use this list to look at jobs in your city or at companies that might have remote offerings and see where there are points of differentiation.
- Leverage resources like PayScale.com to look up salary information for the jobs listed here.
- Use employee review sites like Glassdoor to see what current and former employees are saying about a particular company.
- Stay abreast of the future of work conversations and research by subscribing to updates from the U.S. Labor Statistics and reporting from national publishers covering this area.

About the Author

Sherrell Dorsey is the founder and CEO of The Plug—a venture-backed subscription news and insights platform serving as the Black tech business intelligence source for Fortune 1000 companies, government agencies, and ecosystem leaders across the country. Sherrell's work has been featured in the *Washington Post*, *The Information*, *Fortune* magazine, the *Columbia Journalism Review*, *Vice News*, *Essence*, *Black Enterprise*, and others. *AdWeek* named her one of the top 100 creatives in business in 2021.

Prior to launching The Plug, Dorsey served as a marketing manager for Uber and in sales roles as a contractor on Google Fiber projects. She holds a master's degree in journalism with a concentration in data from Columbia University.

Bibliography

ABS Contributor. "Black Businesses Hire Black People for Two Out of Every Three Jobs." *Atlanta Black Star*, December 22, 2012. https://atlantablackstar.com/2012/12/22/black-businesses-hire-black-people-for-two-out-of-every-three-jobs.

Accenture. "Cloud Computing: Understanding What Cloud Is and What It Can Do for You." Accessed August 3, 2021. https://www.accenture.com/us-en/insights/cloud-computing-index.

Acemoglu, Daron, and Pascual Restrepo. *Robots and Jobs: Evidence from US Labor Markets*. Cambridge, MA: National Bureau of Economic Research, 2017. https://economics.mit.edu/files/19696.

"The African-American Migration Story." *The African Americans: Many Rivers to Cross*. Kunhardt McGee Productions, THIRTEEN Productions LLC, and Inkwell Films (in association with Ark Media). 2013. https://www.pbs.org/wnet/african-americans-many-rivers-to-cross/history/on-african-american-migrations/.

Akhtar, Allana. "Elon Musk Said a College Degree Isn't Required for a Job at Tesla—and Apple, Google, and Netflix Don't Require Employees to Have 4-Year Degrees Either." *Insider*, December 27, 2020. https://www.businessinsider.com/top-companies-are-hiring-more-candidates-without-a-4-year-degree-2019-4.

Allyn, Bobby. "'The Computer Got It Wrong': How Facial Recognition Led to False Arrest of Black Man." NPR, June 24, 2020. https://www.npr.org/2020/06/24/882683463/the-computer-got-it-wrong-how-facial-recognition-led-to-a-false-arrest-in-michig.

Amazon. "As Part of Upskilling 2025, Amazon Is Building on the Success of Its Current Programs as Well as Creating New Training Opportunities for Employees across the U.S." Accessed August 3, 2021. https://www.aboutamazon.com/working-at-amazon/upskilling-2025/upskilling-2025.

Amazon. "Our Workforce Data." Accessed August 3, 2021. https://www.about-amazon.com/news/workplace/our-workforce-data.

Amazon. "Amazon Pledges to Upskill 100,000 U.S. Employees for In-Demand Jobs by 2025." Press release, July 11, 2019. https://press.aboutamazon.com/news-releases/news-release-details/amazon-pledges-upskill-100000-us-employees-demand-jobs-2025.

American Panorama: An Atlas of United States History. "Mapping Inequality: Redlining in New Deal America (map)." Accessed August 3, 2021. https://dsl.richmond.edu/panorama/redlining/#loc=11/47.594/-122.517&city=seattle-wa.

American Psychological Association. "'Bargaining While Black' May Lead to Lower Salaries." Press release, November 7, 2018. https://www.apa.org/news/press/releases/2018/11/bargaining-black.

Anderson, Greta. "Analysis: Students of Color Less Likely to Have Paid Internships." Inside Higher Ed, September 10, 2020. https://www.insidehighered.com/quicktakes/2020/09/10/analysis-students-color-less-likely-have-paid-internships.

Anderson, Monica, and Andrew Perrin. "Disabled Americans Are Less Likely to Use Technology." Pew Research Center, April 7, 2017. https://www.pewresearch.org/fact-tank/2017/04/07/disabled-americans-are-less-likely-to-use-technology/.

Angwin, Julia, and Terry Parris Jr. "Facebook Lets Advertisers Exclude Users by Race: Facebook's System Allows Advertisers to Exclude Black, Hispanic, and Other 'Ethnic Affinities' from Seeing Ads." ProPublica, October 28, 2016. https://www.propublica.org/article/facebook-lets-advertisers-exclude-users-by-race.

Armstrong, Rebecca Lee, and Kevin Parrish. "Are There Programs Available to Help Make Internet Service More Affordable?" HighSpeedInternet.com, May 11, 2021. https://www.highspeedinternet.com/resources/are-there-government-programs-to-help-me-get-internet-service.

Armstrong, Stephen. "The Untold Story of Stripe, the Secretive $20bn Startup Driving Apple, Amazon and Facebook." Wired, May 10, 2018. https://www.wired.co.uk/article/stripe-payments-apple-amazon-facebook.

Asante-Muhammad, Dedrick, Jamie Buell, Talib Graves-Manns, Wilson Lester, and Napoleon Wallace. "Addressing the Needs of Black-Owned Businesses and Entrepreneurs: A Follow-Up Report on the Impacts of COVID-19 on Entrepreneurship in Piedmont, North Carolina." National Community Reinvestment Coalition. Accessed August 3, 2021. https://www.ncrc.org/addressing-the-needs-of-black-owned-businesses-and-entrepreneurs/.

Association for Enterprise Opportunity. "The Tapestry of Black Business Ownership In America: Untapped Opportunities for Success," February 16, 2017. https://community-wealth.org/sites/clone.community-wealth.org/files/downloads/AEO_Black_Owned_Business_Report_02_16_17_FOR_WEB.pdf.

Baboolall, David, Duwain Pinder, Shelley Stewart, and Jason Wright. "Automation and the Future of the African American Workforce." McKinsey & Company, November 14, 2018. https://www.mckinsey.com/featured-insights/future-of-work/automation-and-the-future-of-the-african-american-workforce.

Barroso, Amanda, and Anna Brown. "Gender Pay Gap in U.S. Held Steady in 2020." Pew Research Center, May 25, 2021. https://www.pewresearch.org/fact-tank/2021/05/25/gender-pay-gap-facts/.

Bastian, Rebekah. "The Power of Representation in Leadership Roles." *Forbes*, November 9, 2020. https://www.forbes.com/sites/rebekahbastian/2020/11/09/the-power-of-representation-in-leadership-roles/?sh=5ec1cf496266.

Bayern, Macy. "Top 10 US Universities That Produce the Most Staff for Global Tech Firms." TechRepublic, May 21, 2020. https://www.techrepublic.com/article/top-10-universities-that-produce-the-most-staff-for-global-tech-firms/.

Bedell, Mary S. "Employment and Income of Negro Workers: 1940–52." U.S. Bureau of Labor Statistics, June 1953. https://www.bls.gov/opub/mlr/1953/article/pdf/employment-and-income-of-negro-workers-1940-52.pdf.

Benner, Katie, Glenn Thrush, and Mike Isaac. "Facebook Engages in Housing Discrimination With Its Ad Practices, U.S. Says." *New York Times*, March 28, 2019. https://www.nytimes.com/2019/03/28/us/politics/facebook-housing-discrimination.html.

Bestsennyy, Oleg, Greg Gilbert, Alex Harris, and Jennifer Rost. "Telehealth: A Quarter-Trillion-Dollar Post-COVID-19 Reality?" McKinsey & Company, July 9, 2021. www.mckinsey.com/industries/healthcare-systems-and-services/our-insights/telehealth-a-quarter-trillion-dollar-post-covid-19-reality.

Bhutta, Neil, Andrew C. Chang, Lisa J. Dettling, and Joanne W. Hsu (with assistance from Julia Hewitt). "Disparities in Wealth by Race and Ethnicity in the 2019 Survey of Consumer Finances." FEDS Notes, September 28, 2020. https://www.federalreserve.gov/econres/notes/feds-notes/disparities-in-wealth-by-race-and-ethnicity-in-the-2019-survey-of-consumer-finances-20200928.htm.

BlackBusiness.com. "Top Black Business Magazines, Publications and Blogs." Accessed August 3, 2021. https://www.blackbusiness.com/p/black-business-magazines-publications.html.

BlackPast. "African American Newspapers, Magazines, and Journals." Accessed August 3, 2021. https://www.blackpast.org/special-features/african-american-newspapers/.

Blanco, Lydia. "17 Career Books for Black Women to Help Them Level Up Professionally." *Black Enterprise*, July 14, 2019. https://www.blackenterprise.com/17-career-books-for-black-women/.

Blnded Media. "Are We There Yet? The State of Black Business and The Path to Wealth." February 13, 2019. http://blndedmedia.com/are-we-there-yet/.

Blue Coding. "The Only Tech Podcast List You'll Ever Need (2021 Update)." December 15, 2020. https://www.bluecoding.com/post/the-only-tech-podcast-list-youll-ever-need-2021-update.

Blumberg, Yoni. "Race Doesn't Impact How Job-Seekers Negotiate Salaries—But It Does Affect How Much Money They Get." CNBC, November 13, 2018. https://www.cnbc.com/2018/11/13/study-black-employees-get-lower-offers-during-salary-negotiations.html.

Boston Consulting Group, in partnership with Common Sense and the Southern Education Foundation. *Looking Back, Looking Forward: What It Will Take to Permanently Close the K–12 Digital Divide*. Common Sense Media, 2021. https://www.commonsensemedia.org/sites/default/files/uploads/kids_action/final_-_what_it_will_take_to_permanently_close_the_k-12_digital_divide_vjan26_1.pdf.

Bramble, Sabrina. "Why Representation Matters in Your Workplace and Beyond—Lessons from Wakanda." Mental Health at Work. Accessed August 3, 2021. https://www.mentalhealthatwork.org.uk/blog/why-representation-matters-in-your-workplace-and-beyond-lessons-from-wakanda/.

Break Through Tech. "Chicago." Accessed August 3, 2021. https://www.break-throughtech.org/where-we-work/chicago/.

Brenan, Megan, and Whitney Dupreé. "Representation Shapes Black Employees' Work Experience." Gallup, January 15, 2021. https://news.gallup.com/poll/328457/representation-shapes-black-employees-work-experience.aspx.

Broady, Kristen E., Darlene Booth-Bell, Jason Coupet, and Moriah Macklin. "Race and Jobs at Risk of Being Automated in the Age of COVID-19." Hamilton Project, March 2021. https://www.hamiltonproject.org/assets/files/Automation_LO_v7.pdf.

Busby, John, Julia Tanberk, and BroadbandNow Team. "FCC Reports Broadband Unavailable to 21.3 Million Americans, BroadbandNow Study Indicates 42 Million Do Not Have Access." BroadbandNow Research, May 11, 2021. https://broadbandnow.com/research/fcc-underestimates-unserved-by-50-percent.

Busette, Camille, Jill Simmerman Lawrence, Richard V. Reeves, and Sarah Nzau. "How Social Networks Impact Economic Mobility in Racine, WI, San Francisco, CA, and Washington, DC." Brookings, January, 2021. https://www.brookings.edu/essay/how-we-rise-how-social-networks-impact-economic-mobility-in-racine-wi-san-francisco-ca-and-washington-dc/.

Campbell, Mikey. "Half of New Apple's US Hires in 2018 Lacked 4-Year College Degrees, Cook Says." *Apple Insider*, March 6, 2019. https://appleinsider.com/articles/19/03/06/half-of-new-apples-us-hires-in-2018-lacked-4-year-college-degrees-cook-says.

Carapezza, Kirk. "No College, No Problem: Some Employers Drop Degree Requirements to Diversify Staffs." NPR, *All Things Considered*, April 29, 2021. https://www.npr.org/2021/04/29/990274681/no-college-no-problem-some-employers-drop-degree-requirements-to-diversify-staff.

CB Insights. "Alphabet's Next Billion-Dollar Business: 12 Industries to Watch." June 1, 2021. https://www.cbinsights.com/research/report/industries-disruption-alphabet/.

Centers for Disease Control and Prevention. "Disability Impacts All of Us." Accessed August 3, 2021. https://www.cdc.gov/ncbddd/disabilityandhealth/infographic-disability-impacts-all.html.

Civil Rights & Labor History Consortium. "Mapping Race and Segregation in Seattle and King County 1940–2019." Accessed August 3, 2021. http://depts.washington.edu/labhist/maps-race-seattle.shtml.

Cohen, Josh. "'Where Are the Black People?' Central District Residents Get Creative to Fight Displacement." Crosscut, January 25, 2019. https://crosscut.com/2019/01/where-are-black-people-central-district-residents-get-creative-fight-displacement.

Coney, Cheryl M. "Overcoming Barriers: Black Women at Boeing." UW Tacoma Digital Commons, Fall 2013. https://digitalcommons.tacoma.uw.edu/cgi/viewcontent.cgi?article=1015&context=ias_masters.

Connley, Courtney. "Google, Apple and 12 Other Companies That No Longer Require Employees to Have a College Degree." CNBC, October 8, 2018. https://www.cnbc.com/2018/08/16/15-companies-that-no-longer-require-employees-to-have-a-college-degree.html.

Conversation, The. "Why Black and Hispanic Small-Business Owners Have Been So Badly Hit in the Pandemic Recession." February 23, 2021. https://theconversation.com/why-black-and-hispanic-small-business-owners-have-been-so-badly-hit-in-the-pandemic-recession-150818.

Corrales, Ana. "New Tools to Help Spanish Speakers Build Their Careers." Google, August 21, 2019. https://blog.google/outreach-initiatives/grow-with-google/spanish-language-tools/.

Courtney, Emily. "30 Companies Switching to Long-Term Remote Work." Flexjobs. Accessed August 3, 2021. https://www.flexjobs.com/blog/post/companies-switching-remote-work-long-term/.

Dastin, Jeffrey. "Amazon Scraps Secret AI Recruiting Tool That Showed Bias Against Women." Reuters, October 10, 2018. https://www.reuters.com/article/us-amazon-com-jobs-automation-insight/amazon-scraps-secret-ai-recruiting-tool-that-showed-bias-against-women-idUSKCN1MK08G.

Daxx. "What's the Engineer Salary in Silicon Valley and Where to Hire Programmers for Lower Rates?" May 20, 2021. https://www.daxx.com/blog/development-trends/average-engineer-salary-silicon-valley.

Day, Matt. "Ten Years Ago, Amazon Changed Seattle, Announcing Its Move to South Lake Union." *Seattle Times*, December 21, 2017. https://www .seattletimes.com/business/amazon/ten-years-ago-amazon-changed-seattle-announcing-its-move-to-south-lake-union/.

Deloitte. "Quantifying the Economic Impact of Closing the Digital Divide." Press release, May 3, 2021. https://www2.deloitte.com/us/en/pages/about-deloitte/articles/press-releases/quantifying-the-economic-impact-of-closing-the-digital-divide.html.

DeRuy, Emily, and National Journal. "Are Unpaid Internships Barriers to Success for Some Students of Color?" *The Atlantic*, July 8, 2015. https://www.theatlantic.com/politics/archive/2015/07/are-unpaid-internships-barriers-to-success-for-some-students-of-color/432255/.

Desjardins, Jeff. "How Much Data Is Generated Each Day?" World Economic Forum, April 17, 2019. https://www.weforum.org/agenda/2019/04/how-much-data-is-generated-each-day-cf4bddf29f/.

Dice. *Dice Q1 Tech Job Report: The Fastest-Growing Hubs, Roles and Skills.* 2021. https://marketing.dice.com/pdf/2021/Dice_Q1_Tech_Job_Report.pdf.

Dignan, Larry. "Top Cloud Providers in 2021: AWS, Microsoft Azure, and Google Cloud, Hybrid, SaaS Players." *ZDNet*, April 2, 2021. https://www.zdnet.com/article/the-top-cloud-providers-of-2021-aws-microsoft-azure-google-cloud-hybrid-saas/.

Dishman, Lydia. "Black Tech Workers Are the Lowest Paid in the Industry." *Fast Company*, February 8, 2018. https://www.fastcompany.com/40528496/black-tech-workers-are-the-lowest-paid-in-the-industry.

The Divide. "Dr. Nicol Turner Lee on the 'Digitally Invisible'" [podcast]. Light-Reading, February 2, 2021. https://www.lightreading.com/opticalip/fttx/podcast---divide-dr-nicol-turner-lee-on-digitally-invisible/v/d-id/767278.

Dixon, Amanda. "Survey: Nearly 1 in 3 Side Hustlers Needs the Income to Stay Afloat." Bankrate, June 5, 2019. https://www.bankrate.com/personal-finance/side-hustles-survey-june-2019/.

Downs, Kenya. "African-Americans Over-Represented among Low-Paying College Majors." PBS News Hour, February 9, 2016. https://www.pbs.org/newshour/education/african-americans-over-represented-among-low-paying-college-majors.

Eubanks, Virginia. *Automating Inequality: How High-Tech Tools Profile, Police, and Punish the Poor.* New York: Picador, 2019.

Fairlie, Robert. "COVID-19, Small Business Owners, and Racial Inequality." *The Reporter* 4 (2020). https://www.nber.org/reporter/2020number4/covid-19-small-business-owners-and-racial-inequality.

Feedspot. "Top 60 Technology Podcasts You Must Follow in 2021." Last updated July 29, 2021. https://blog.feedspot.com/technology_podcasts/.

Galbraith, Diane, and Sunita Mondal. "The Potential Power of Internships and the Impact on Career Preparation." *Research in Higher Education Journal* 38 (2020). https://files.eric.ed.gov/fulltext/EJ1263677.pdf.

Gates, Dominic. "Boeing's Difficult Journey from Racism to Diversity." *Seattle Times*, January 16, 2017. https://www.seattletimes.com/business/boeing-aerospace/boeings-difficult-journey-from-racism-to-diversity/.

Gibson, Kate. "U.S. to Erase $1 Billion in Debt for Students Scammed by For-Profit Colleges." CBS News, March 18, 2021. https://www.cbsnews.com/news/student-debt-for-profit-college-forgiveness-1-billion/.

Glantz, Aaron, and Emmanuel Martinez. "For People of Color, Banks Are Shutting the Door to Homeownership." Reveal, February 15, 2018. https://revealnews.org/article/for-people-of-color-banks-are-shutting-the-door-to-homeownership/.

Glassdoor Team. "Do Race & Gender Play a Role in Salary Negotiations? A New Study Says Yes." Glassdoor, October 17, 2016. https://www.glassdoor.com/blog/do-race-gender-play-a-role-in-salary-negotiations/.

Global Digital Literacy Council. "Signing and Ratification of the Global Standard 6." Accessed August 3, 2021. https://www.gdlcouncil.org/.

Goodwill. "About Us." Accessed August 3, 2021. https://www.goodwill.org/about-us/.

Goodwill Industries of the Southern Piedmont. "Information Technology Training." Accessed August 3, 2021. https://goodwillsp.org/train/goodwill-university/it-training/.

Greig, Jonathan. "Coding Bootcamps and 4-Year Colleges Have Nearly Identical Percentage of Alumni Employed at Big Five: Report." *ZDNet*, June 11, 2021. https://www.zdnet.com/article/coding-bootcamps-and-4-year-colleges-have-nearly-identical-percentage-of-alumni-employed-at-big-five-report/.

Guilford, Gwynn. "Black Income Is Half That of White Households in the US—Just Like It Was in the 1950s." *Quartz*, September 1, 2018. https://qz.com/1368251/black-income-is-half-that-of-white-households-just-like-it-was-in-the-1950s/.

Hanson, Melanie. "Student Loan Debt Statistics." EducationData.org, updated July 10, 2021. https://educationdata.org/student-loan-debt-statistics.

Harris, Leslie M. "The Long, Ugly History of Racism at American Universities." *New Republic*, March 26, 2015. https://newrepublic.com/article/121382/forgotten-racist-past-american-universities.

Haselton, Todd. "How to Borrow Free Audiobooks from Your Local Library on Your Phone." CNBC, July 25, 2018. https://www.cnbc.com/2018/07/25/how-to-borrow-audiobooks-from-library-on-phone-using-libby-app.html.

Helhoski, Anna, and Ryan Lane. "Student Loan Debt Statistics: 2021; U.S. Student Loan Debt Totals $1.6 Trillion as of March 31, 2021." Nerdwallet, July 15, 2021. https://www.nerdwallet.com/article/loans/student-loans/student-loan-debt.

Henry. "Every Company Going Remote Permanently: Jul 29, 2021 Update." BuildRemote, July 29, 2021. https://buildremote.co/companies/companies-going-remote-permanently/.

Hess, Abigail Johnson. "The Pandemic Accelerated Job Automation and Black and Latino Workers Are Most Likely to Be Replaced." CNBC, March 17, 2021. https://www.cnbc.com/2021/03/17/black-latino-workers-most-likely-to-be-replaced-by-automation-report.html.

Hess, Abigail Johnson. "This Tech Company Has the Most Highly-Educated Employees." CNBC, July 28, 2017. https://www.cnbc.com/2017/07/28/this-tech-company-has-the-most-highly-educated-employees.html.

Hickson, Ally. "This Google Employee Is Living in a Truck & Saving SO MUCH Money." Refinery29, October 20, 2015. https://www.refinery29.com/en-us/2015/10/96088/google-employee-living-in-truck.

Hightower, Chelsea D. "Exploring the Role of Gender and Race in Salary Negotiations." Master's thesis, Louisiana State University, 2019. https://digitalcommons.lsu.edu/cgi/viewcontent.cgi?article=5986&context=gradschool_theses.

Hired. "State of Salaries Report: Data Reveals Where Techies Get Paid Most and the Skills That Get Them There." Accessed August 3, 2021. https://hired.com/state-of-salaries-2018#black-tech-shortchanged?cookie_consent=true.

HistoryLink.org staff. "Boeing Hires Florise Spearman, First African American Employee, in January 1942." HistoryLink.org, December 28, 2000. https://historylink.org/File/2916.

IBM. "IBM Launches Free, Open Digital Learning Platform 'SkillsBuild Reignite' to Help Canadian Job Seekers and Business Owners Get Back to Work." Cision, July 27, 2020. https://www.newswire.ca/news-releases/ibm-launches-free-open-digital-learning-platform-skillsbuild-reignite-to-help-canadian-job-seekers-and-business-owners-get-back-to-work-811150034.html.

IBM. "What Is Automation?" Accessed August 3, 2021. https://www.ibm.com/topics/automation.

IBM. The Enterprise Guide to Closing the Skills Gap: Strategies for Building and Maintaining a Skilled Workforce. n.d. IBM Institute for Business Value. https://www.ibm.com/downloads/cas/EPYMNBJA.

IBM Cloud Education. "Machine Learning." IBM, July 15, 2020. https://www.ibm.com/cloud/learn/machine-learning.

Indeed Editorial Team. "Do Interns Get Paid?" Indeed, February 22, 2021. https://www.indeed.com/career-advice/pay-salary/do-interns-get-paid.

Jan, Tracy. "Redlining Was Banned 50 Years Ago: It's Still Hurting Minorities Today." Washington Post, March 28, 2018. https://www.washingtonpost.com/news/wonk/wp/2018/03/28/redlining-was-banned-50-years-ago-its-still-hurting-minorities-today/.

Jara, Adriana. "Helping Latino Students Learn to Code." Google, March 19, 2019. https://www.blog.google/outreach-initiatives/google-org/computer-science-lessons-spanish/.

Jim, Trevor. "John Reynolds and the Invention of Pattern Matching" [blog]. May 27, 2013. http://trevorjim.com/john-reynolds-and-the-invention-of-pattern-matching/.

Joho, Jess. "The 18 Best Tech Podcasts (That Aren't 'Reply All'): Here's a Super Tech Support for Finding Other Great Tech Podcasts." *Mashable*, April 11, 2021. https://mashable.com/article/best-tech-podcasts-reply-all-alternatives.

JPMorgan Chase & Co. "The Online Platform Economy in 2018: Drivers, Workers, Sellers, and Lessors; Finding Five: Participation Rates in the Online Platform Economy Varied Significantly across the Nation." Accessed August 3, 2021. https://www.jpmorganchase.com/institute/research/labor-markets/report-ope-2018.htm#finding-5.

Kapor Center. "Diversity Data Shows Need to Focus on Women of Color." First published on *Huffington Post*, July 9, 2014. https://www.kaporcenter.org/diversity-data-shows-need-to-focus-on-women-of-color/.

Kauffman Indicators of Entrepreneurship. *State Report on Early-Stage Entrepreneurship in the United States: 2020*. March, 2021. https://indicators.kauffman.org/wp-content/uploads/sites/2/2021/03/2020_Early-Stage-Entrepreneurship-State-Report.pdf.

Kelly, Heather, and Rachel Lerman. "As Offices Open Back Up, Not All Tech Companies Are Sold on a Remote Future." *Washington Post*, June 4, 2021. https://www.washingtonpost.com/technology/2021/06/04/big-tech-office-openings/.

Khalid, Amrita. "America's Digital Divide Is Even More Urgent During the Pandemic." *Quartz*, April 9, 2020. https://qz.com/1836040/americas-digital-divide-is-more-urgent-during-a-pandemic/.

Kidwai, Aman. "How COVID-19 Improved Accessibility for Job Seekers with Disabilities: The Expansion of Remote Work and Recruiting Technology Is Leveling the Playing Field at Work, Experts Told HR Dive." HR Dive, July 17, 2020. https://www.hrdive.com/news/how-covid-19-improved-accessibility-for-job-seekers-with-disabilities/581820/.

Klobuchar, Amy. "Klobuchar, Clyburn Introduce Comprehensive Broadband Infrastructure Legislation to Expand Access to Affordable High-Speed Internet." Press release, March 11, 2021. https://www.klobuchar.senate.gov/public/index.cfm/2021/3/klobuchar-clyburn-introduce-comprehensive-broadband-infrastructure-legislation-to-expand-access-to-affordable-high-speed-internet.

Kochhar, Rakesh. "Latinos' Incomes Higher Than Before Great Recession, but U.S.-Born Latinos Yet to Recover." Pew Research Center, March 7, 2019. https://www.pewresearch.org/hispanic/2019/03/07/latinos-incomes-higher-than-before-great-recession-but-u-s-born-latinos-yet-to-recover/.

Koksal, Ilker. "The Rise of Online Learning." *Forbes*, May 2, 2020. https://www.forbes.com/sites/ilkerkoksal/2020/05/02/the-rise-of-online-learning/?sh=369c77e572f3.

Koonin, Lisa M., et al. "Trends in the Use of Telehealth During the Emergence of the COVID-19 Pandemic—United States, January–March 2020." Centers for Disease Control and Prevention, October 30, 2020. https://www.cdc.gov/mmwr/volumes/69/wr/mm6943a3.htm.

Landsman, Stephanie. "What College Tuition Will Look Like in 18 Years." CNBC.com, May 25, 2012. https://www.cnbc.com/id/47565202.

Lawler, Ryan. "Stripe Opens Its Atlas Program to US-Based Startups." TechCrunch, April 6, 2017. https://techcrunch.com/2017/04/06/stripe-atlas-us/.

Lee, Michelle. "Black History STEAM Book List for Kids, Teens & Adults." New York Public Library, February 1, 2021. https://www.nypl.org/blog/2021/02/01/black-history-steam-booklist.

Lee, Yejin. "Mentorship as a Tool for Growth, Inclusion, and Equity." Idealist, January 6, 2020. https://www.idealist.org/en/careers/mentorship-diversity-inclusion.

Leonhardt, Megan. "60% of Women Say They've Never Negotiated Their Salary—and Many Quit Their Job Instead." CNBC, January 31, 2020. https://www.cnbc.com/2020/01/31/women-more-likely-to-change-jobs-to-get-pay-increase.html.

Library of Congress. "Audio Books." Accessed August 3, 2021. https://guides.loc.gov/e-books/audio-books.

Library of Congress. "Library of Congress E-Books." Accessed August 3, 2021. https://guides.loc.gov/en/books/library-congress.

Lieberman, Mark. "New York Banned Facial Recognition in Schools. Will Other States Follow?" EducationWeek, December 30, 2020. https://www.edweek.org/technology/new-york-banned-facial-recognition-in-schools-will-other-states-follow/2020/12.

Long, Katherine. "The Deed to Your Seattle-Area Home May Contain Racist Language: Here's How to Fix It." Seattle Times, January 7, 2019. https://www.seattletimes.com/seattle-news/the-deed-to-your-house-may-contain-racist-covenants-heres-how-to-fix-it/.

Lorenz, Taylor. "The Original Renegade." New York Times, February 13, 2020. https://www.nytimes.com/2020/02/13/style/the-original-renegade.html.

McCarthy, Niall. "The U.S. Cities with the Most Homeless People." Statista, April 16, 2021. https://www.statista.com/chart/6949/the-us-cities-with-the-most-homeless-people/.

McCarthy, Niall. "Where U.S. Tech Workers Get Paid the Most [Infographic]." Forbes, June 17, 2020. https://www.forbes.com/sites/niallmccarthy/2020/06/17/where-us-tech-workers-get-paid-the-most-infographic/?sh=3fe960541f98.

McIntosh, Kriston, Emily Moss, Ryan Nunn, and Jay Shambaugh. "Examining the Black-White Wealth Gap." Brookings, February 27, 2020. https://www.brookings.edu/blog/up-front/2020/02/27/examining-the-black-white-wealth-gap/.

McIntyre, Lindsay-Rae. "Microsoft's 2020 Diversity & Inclusion Report: A Commitment to Accelerate Progress amidst Global Change." Microsoft, October 21, 2020. https://blogs.microsoft.com/blog/2020/10/21/microsofts-2020-diversity-inclusion-report-a-commitment-to-accelerate-progress-amidst-global-change/.

McKinsey & Company. "Building Supportive Ecosystems for Black-Owned US Businesses." October 29, 2020. https://www.mckinsey.com/industries/public-and-social-sector/our-insights/building-supportive-ecosystems-for-black-owned-us-businesses.

McKinsey & Company. "The Economic Impact of Closing the Racial Wealth Gap." August 13, 2019. https://www.mckinsey.com/industries/public-sector/our-insights/the-economic-impact-of-closing-the-racial-wealth-gap.

McKinsey & Company. "Women in the Workplace 2020." September 30, 2020. https://www.mckinsey.com/featured-insights/diversity-and-inclusion/women-in-the-workplace.

McKinsey Global Institute. "The Economic State of Black America: What Is and What Could Be." June 17, 2021. https://www.mckinsey.com/featured-insights/diversity-and-inclusion/the-economic-state-of-black-america-what-is-and-what-could-be.

Melton, Monica. "One in Three Black Founders with $1 Million+ in Venture Capital Graduated from a Black Accelerator." The Plug, January 11, 2021. https://tpinsights.com/2021/01/11/one-in-three-black-founders-with-1-million-in-venture-capital-graduated-from-a-black-accelerator/.

Microsoft. "Blacks at Microsoft Scholarship." Accessed August 3, 2021. https://www.microsoft.com/en-us/diversity/programs/blacks-scholarships.aspx.

Microsoft. *Global Diversity & Inclusion Report* 2020. 2021. https://query.prod.cms.rt.microsoft.com/cms/api/am/binary/RE4H2f8.

Microsoft. "Intern Programme." Accessed August 3, 2021. https://www.microsoft.com/en-ie/earlycareers/internsapprenticeships.

Microsoft. "Microsoft in Education Fact Sheet." March 12, 2008. https://news.microsoft.com/2008/03/12/microsoft-in-education-fact-sheet.

Miller, Ron. "Tech Companies Are Looking at More Flexible Work Models When Offices Reopen." *TechCrunch*, June 11, 2021. https://techcrunch.com/2021/06/11/tech-companies-are-looking-at-more-flexible-work-models-when-offices-reopen/.

Muro, Mark, Robert Maxim, and Jacob Whiton. "Automation and Artificial Intelligence: How Machines Are Affecting People and Places." Brookings, January 24, 2019. https://www.brookings.edu/research/automation-and-artificial-intelligence-how-machines-affect-people-and-places/.

Natanson, Hannah, Valerie Strauss, and Katherine Frey. "How America Failed Students with Disabilities During the Pandemic." *Washington Post*, May 20, 2021. https://www.washingtonpost.com/education/2021/05/20/students-disabilities-virtual-learning-failure/.

National Agricultural Library. "Collections." U.S. Department of Agriculture. Accessed August 3, 2021. https://www.nal.usda.gov/main/collections.

National Center for Education Evaluation and Regional Assistance. "What's New at NCEE." Institute of Education Sciences. Accessed August 3, 2021. https://ies.ed.gov/ncee/.

National Partnership for Women & Families. "Quantifying America's Gender Wage Gap by Race/Ethnicity." March 2021. https://www.nationalpartnership.org/our-work/resources/economic-justice/fair-pay/quantifying-americas-gender-wage-gap.pdf.

National Transportation Library. "Research Tools." U.S. Department of Transportation. Accessed August 3, 2021. https://transportation.libguides.com/researchtools.

Ndung'u, Njuguna, and Landry Signé. "The Fourth Industrial Revolution and Digitization Will Transform Africa into a Global Powerhouse." Brookings, January 8, 2020. https://www.brookings.edu/research/the-fourth-industrial-revolution-and-digitization-will-transform-africa-into-a-global-powerhouse/.

Nelson, Libby. "College Could Cost Up to $100,000 per Year by 2030: Here's How to Save." Vox, August 28, 2015. https://www.vox.com/personal-finance/2015/8/28/9217075/save-for-college.

Nevada Today. "Eight Business Students Intern with Microsoft Licensing, GP." August 8, 2008. https://www.unr.edu/nevada-today/news/2008/eight-business-students-intern-with-microsoft-licensing-gp.

Nickelsburg, Monica. "Tech Companies Are Doubling Down on Family Leave to Improve Recruiting and Diversity." GeekWire, April 24, 2019. https://www.geekwire.com/2019/tech-companies-doubling-family-leave-improve-recruiting-diversity/.

Nicoll, Alex. "Homeless Parents' Lawsuit Forcing New York City to Provide WiFi for 114,000 Homeless Students Will Head to Trial." Insider, January 3, 2021. https://www.businessinsider.com/lawsuit-to-provide-wifi-to-homeless-nyc-students-moves-forward-2021-1?utm_source=newsletter&utm_medium=email&utm_campaign=cb_bureau_ny.

O'Donnell, Bob. "Looking to Level Up? Amazon, Google, Microsoft and More Offer Training Programs." USA Today, April 26, 2021. https://eu.usatoday.com/story/tech/columnist/2021/04/26/amazon-google-and-more-offer-training-programs-newcomers/7335646002/.

Office of Advocacy. "Small Businesses Drive Job Growth in United States; They Account for 1.8 Million Net New Jobs, Latest Data Show." U.S. Small Business Administration, April 24, 2019. https://advocacy.sba.gov/2019/04/24/small-businesses-drive-job-growth-in-united-states-they-account-for-1-8-million-net-new-jobs-latest-data-show/.

Office of the City Clerk, Seattle. "Seattle's Community Profile." Accessed August 3, 2021. http://clerk.seattle.gov/~ordpics/115018_%20Doc%202%20-%20Community%20Profile%20-%20Demographic%20Trends.htm.

Office of Planning and Community Development, Seattle. "Neighborhood Change: Part of the Equitable Development Monitoring Program." Accessed August 3, 2021. https://population-and-demographics-seattlecitygis.hub.arcgis.com/pages/neighborhood-change.

Ortutay, Barbara. "What Does an Engineer Look Like?" *Smithsonian TweenTrib-une*, August 12, 2015. https://www.tweentribune.com/article/tween56/what-does-engineer-look/.

Parker, Kim, and Richard Fry. "More Than Half of U.S. Households Have Some Investment in the Stock Market." Pew Research Center, March 25, 2020. https://www.pewresearch.org/fact-tank/2020/03/25/more-than-half-of-u-s-households-have-some-investment-in-the-stock-market/.

Parker, Melonie. "Digital Skills Training for 100,000 Black Women." Google, February 12, 2021. https://blog.google/outreach-initiatives/grow-with-google/black-women-lead/.

Pasqua, Marco, "How COVID-19 Is Changing Remote Work for People with Disabilities." Rich Hansen Foundation, April 9, 2020. https://www.rick-hansen.com/news-stories/blog/how-covid-19-changing-remote-work-people-disabilities.

Patten, Eileen. "Racial, Gender Wage Gaps Persist in U.S. Despite Some Progress." Pew Research Center, July 1, 2016. https://www.pewresearch.org/fact-tank/2016/07/01/racial-gender-wage-gaps-persist-in-u-s-despite-some-progress/.

Payscale. "The State of the Gender Pay Gap in 2021." Accessed August 3, 2021. https://www.payscale.com/data/gender-pay-gap.

Perry, Andre M., and Carl Romer. "To Expand the Economy, Invest in Black Businesses." Brookings, December 31, 2020. https://www.brookings.edu/essay/to-expand-the-economy-invest-in-black-businesses/.

Pew Research Center. "Mobile Fact Sheet." April 7, 2021. https://www.pewresearch.org/internet/fact-sheet/mobile/.

PON staff. "Counteracting Negotiation Biases Like Race and Gender in the Workplace." Harvard Law School, Program on Negotiation, November 19, 2020. https://www.pon.harvard.edu/daily/leadership-skills-daily/counteracting-racial-and-gender-bias-in-job-negotiations-nb/.

Poon, Linda. "Where the U.S. Underestimates the Digital Divide." Bloomberg CityLab, February 19, 2020. https://www.bloomberg.com/news/articles/2020-02-19/where-the-u-s-underestimates-the-digital-divide?sref=Rqh286j3.

Project on Predatory Student Lending. "For-Profit College Students File Lawsuit to Force Betsy Devos to Follow the Law and Cancel Their Student Loan Debt" [press release]. Legal Services Center of Harvard Law School, June 25, 2019. https://predatorystudentlending.org/news/press-releases/defrauded-for-profit-college-students-file-lawsuit-to-force-betsy-devos-cancel-student-loan-debt-borrower-defense/.

Prosperity Now. "The Racial Wealth Divide in Seattle, WA." March 2021. https://prosperitynow.org/sites/default/files/Racial%20Wealth%20Divide_%20Profile_Seattle_FINAL_3.2.21.pdf.

PwC. "PwC Network Invests $3bn Globally in Digital Training and Technology to Support Clients and Communities." Press release, November 5, 2019. https://www.pwc.com/bb/en/press-releases/2019/3bn-investment-in-digital-upskilling.pdf.

Qualcomm. "Everything You Need to Know About 5G." Accessed August 3, 2021. https://www.qualcomm.com/5g/what-is-5g.

Rascouët-Paz, Anna. "Mapping Out the U.S. Digital Divide: Nicol Turner-Lee." Shot of Science from *Annual Reviews*, April 30, 2020. https://www.annual-reviews.org/shot-of-science/multimedia/mapping-digital-divide.

Reaume, Amanda. "How Much College Will Cost in 5, 10 & 15 Years." Northwestern Mutual, July 9, 2020. https://www.northwesternmutual.com/life-and-money/how-much-college-will-cost-in-5-10-and-15-years/.

Recruiting Innovation. "Diversity in Tech: We've Got a Long Way to Go." Accessed August 3, 2021. https://recruitinginnovation.com/blog/diversity-in-tech/.

Rhee, Sung. "Coding Bootcamp vs College: Which Will Help You Land the Most Prestigious Jobs in the Tech Industry?" Switchup, May 11, 2021 [last updated]. https://www.switchup.org/blog/coding-bootcamps-vs-college-for-prestigious-tech-jobs.

Richards, Erin, Elinor Aspegren, and Erin Mansfield. "A Year into the Pandemic, Thousands of Students Still Can't Get Reliable WiFi for School: The Digital Divide Remains Worse Than Ever." *USA Today*, February 4, 2021. https://www.usatoday.com/story/news/education/2021/02/04/covid-online-school-broadband-internet-laptops/3930744001/.

Rose, Lydia. "The Digital Edge: How Black and Latino Youth Navigate Digital Inequality by S. Craig Watkins et al. (review)." *Social Forces* 98, no. 1 (2019), e4. https://muse.jhu.edu/article/748378.

Rosenthal, Rachel. "Tech Companies Want You to Believe America Has a Skills Gap." *Bloomberg*, August 4, 2020. https://www.bloomberg.com/opinion/articles/2020-08-04/big-tech-wants-you-to-believe-america-has-a-skills-gap?sref=Rqh286j3.

Salter, Nicholas. "The Importance of Minority Leader Representation." Ohio State University Fisher College of Business, February 27, 2019. https://fisher.osu.edu/blogs/leadreadtoday/blog/the-importance-of-minority-leader-representation.

Schaeffer, Katherine. "As Schools Shift to Online Learning Amid Pandemic, Here's What We Know About Disabled Students in the U.S." Pew Research Center, April 23, 2020. https://www.pewresearch.org/fact-tank/2020/04/23/as-schools-shift-to-online-learning-amid-pandemic-heres-what-we-know-about-disabled-students-in-the-u-s/.

Schur, L.A., M. Ameri, and D. Kruse. "Telework After COVID: A 'Silver Lining' for Workers with Disabilities?" *Journal of Occupational Rehabilitation* 30 (2020): 521–536. https://link.springer.com/article/10.1007/s10926-020-09936-5.

Scott, Ellen. "Woman Who Earns Over $300,000 a Year Chooses to Live in a Van." *Metro*, June 23, 2021. https://metro.co.uk/2021/06/23/woman-who-earns-over-300000-a-year-chooses-to-live-in-a-van-14817342/.

Seattle Civil Rights & Labor History Project. "Racial Restrictive Covenants Map Seattle/King County." Accessed August 3, 2021. https://depts.washington.edu/civilr/covenants_map.htm.

Seattle Civil Rights & Labor History Project. "Racial Restrictive Covenants: Neighborhood by Neighborhood Restrictions across King County." Accessed August 3, 2021. https://depts.washington.edu/civilr/covenants.htm.

Seattle Foundation. "Blacks at Microsoft Scholarship." Accessed August 3, 2021. https://seattlefoundation.smapply.org/prog/blacks_at_microsoft_scholarship/.

Seattle Office of Planning & Community Development. *Equitable Development Community Indicators Report*. September 2020. https://www.seattle.gov/Documents/Departments/OPCD/Demographics/communityindicatorsreport2020.pdf.

"Seattle's Ugly Past: Segregation in Our Neighborhoods." *Seattle Magazine*, March 2013. https://www.seattlemag.com/article/seattles-ugly-past-segregation-our-neighborhoods.

Silva, Catherine. "Racial Restrictive Covenants History: Enforcing Neighborhood Segregation in Seattle." Seattle Civil Rights & Labor History Project. Accessed August 3, 2021. https://depts.washington.edu/civilr/covenants_report.htm.

Smith, Noah. "Clean-Tech Investment Isn't Just a Bubble This Time." *Bloomberg*, March 18, 2021. https://www.bloomberg.com/opinion/articles/2021-03-18/clean-tech-investment-isn-t-just-a-bubble-this-time?sref=Rqh286j3.

Smith, Rachel. "CORE's Drive for Equal Employment in Downtown Seattle." Seattle Civil Rights & Labor History Project. Accessed August 3, 2021. https://depts.washington.edu/civilr/core_deeds.htm.

Smith, Trevor. "How Unpaid Internships Reinforce the Racial Wealth Gap." *The American Prospect*, February 4, 2019. https://prospect.org/education/unpaid-internships-reinforce-racial-wealth-gap/.

Southern, Matt. "Google Opens Enrollment for Career Certification Courses." *Search Engine Journal*, March 11, 2021. https://www.searchenginejournal.com/google-opens-enrollment-for-career-certification-courses/398774/#close.

Stanford University. "Defining AI." Accessed August 3, 2021. https://ai100.stanford.edu/2016-report/section-i-what-artificial-intelligence/defining-ai.

Statista. "Number of Amazon.com Employees from 2007 to 2020." Accessed August 3, 2021. https://www.statista.com/statistics/234488/number-of-amazon-employees/.

Stoll, Michael A., Steven Raphael, and Harry J. Holzer. "Why Are Black Employers More Likely Than White Employers to Hire Blacks?" Discussion Paper, distributed by ERIC Clearinghouse, August 2001. https://www.irp.wisc.edu/publications/dps/pdfs/dp123601.pdf.

Stripe. "Announcing Stripe Atlas—Helping Entrepreneurs Start a Global Business from Anywhere." Press release, February 24, 2016. https://stripe.com/newsroom/news/stripe-launches-atlas.

Subin, Samantha. "Tech Executives Are Rethinking How to Hire for In-Demand Jobs: Survey." CNBC, March 25, 2021. https://www.cnbc.com/2021/03/25/tech-executives-rethink-how-to-hire-for-in-demand-jobs.html.

Sweet et al v. DeVos et al., N.D. Cal Case No. 19-cv-03674 (2019). https://predatorystudentlending.org/wp-content/uploads/2019/06/Complaint.pdf.

Tate, Cassandra. "YMCA—East Madison Branch." HistoryLink.org, March 31, 2001. https://www.historylink.org/file/3152.

Tayeb, Zahra. "From Permanent Work-from-Home Models to Full-Scale Returns, Companies Like Amazon, Twitter, and Goldman Sachs Are Pursuing Different Office Policies as Restrictions Ease." Insider, June 16, 2021. https://www.businessinsider.com/remote-working-divide-amazon-twitter-goldman-spotify-hybrid-offices-2021-3.

Techopedia. "Pattern Matching." Last updated June 13, 2018. Accessed August 3, 2021. https://www.techopedia.com/definition/8801/pattern-matching.

Thoughts from Inside the Box. "About Me." Accessed August 3, 2021. https://frominsidethebox.com/about.

Thoughts from Inside the Box. "The Reality." May 23, 2015. https://frominsidethebox.com/view?key=5741031244955648.

U.S. Bureau of Labor Statistics. "Occupational Outlook Handbook: Software Developers, Quality Assurance Analysts, and Testers." Accessed August 3, 2021. https://www.bls.gov/ooh/computer-and-information-technology/software-developers.htm.

U.S. Census Bureau. "Income of Families and Persons in the United States: 1950." Report Number P60-09, March 25, 1952. https://www.census.gov/library/publications/1952/demo/p60-009.html.

U.S. Congress. "Accessible, Affordable Internet for All Act." H.R.1783, 117th Congress. https://www.congress.gov/bill/117th-congress/house-bill/1783/text.

U.S. Department of Labor. "Fact Sheet #71: Internship Programs Under The Fair Labor Standards Act." Updated January 2018. https://www.dol.gov/agencies/whd/fact-sheets/71-flsa-internships.

U.S. Department of Labor. "The Boeing Co. (Washington Plants): 1936–67." Bulletin No. 1565, August 1967. https://fraser.stlouisfed.org/files/docs/publications/bls/bls_1565_1967.pdf.

U.S. Equal Employment Opportunity Commission. "Diversity in High Tech." Accessed August 3, 2021. https://www.eeoc.gov/special-report/diversity-high-tech.

University of Minnesota Libraries: Mapping Prejudice. "What Are Covenants?" Accessed August 3, 2021. https://mappingprejudice.umn.edu/what-are-covenants/.

USA Facts. "4.4 Million Households with Children Don't Have Consistent Access to Computers for Online Learning During the Pandemic." September 28, 2020 (updated October 19, 2020). https://usafacts.org/articles/internet-access-students-at-home/.

Uzialko, Adam. "Workplace Automation Is Everywhere, and It's Not Just About Robots." *Business News Daily*, updated February 26, 2019. https://www.businessnewsdaily.com/9835-automation-tech-workforce.html.

Valenti, Denise. "Benjamin's 'Race After Technology' Speaks to a Growing Concern among Many of Tech Bias." Princeton University, May 15, 2020. https://www.princeton.edu/news/2020/05/15/benjamins-race-after-technology-speaks-growing-concern-among-many-tech-bias.

Varghese, Sanjana. "Ruha Benjamin: 'We Definitely Can't Wait for Silicon Valley to Become More Diverse.'" *Guardian*, June 29, 2019. https://www.theguardian.com/technology/2019/jun/29/ruha-benjamin-we-cant-wait-silicon-valley-become-more-diverse-prejudice-algorithms-data-new-jim-code.

Venator, Joanna, and Richard V. Reeves. "Unpaid Internships: Support Beams for the Glass Floor." Brookings, July 7, 2015. https://www.brookings.edu/blog/social-mobility-memos/2015/07/07/unpaid-internships-support-beams-for-the-glass-floor/.

Verizon. "It's a New Day at Work." Accessed August 3, 2021. https://www.verizon.com/about/responsibility/human-prosperity/reskilling-program.

Vitalis, Ignas. "US Demographics and the Stock Market." Tradimo News, October 25, 2019. https://news.tradimo.com/us-demographics-and-the-stock-market/.

Watt, Mary Ann, with Christopher Zinkowicz et al. "African American Occupations in the 1900s." Berks History Center. Accessed August 3, 2021. https://www.berkshistory.org/multimedia/articles/african-american-occupations-in-the-1900s/.

"Why Google Believes You Don't Need a College Degree to Get a High Paying Tech Job." *Analytics India Magazine*, November 8, 2020. https://analyticsindiamag.com/why-google-believes-you-dont-need-a-college-degree-to-get-a-high-paying-tech-job/.

Wikipedia. "Microsoft Redmond Campus." Last modified April 17, 2021. https://en.wikipedia.org/wiki/Microsoft_Redmond_campus.

Wikipedia. "Second Great Migration (African American)." Last modified June 21, 2021. https://en.wikipedia.org/wiki/Second_Great_Migration_(African_American)#cite_note-7.

Wired staff. "The Rise and Rise of the Redmond Empire." *Wired*, December 1, 1998. https://www.wired.com/1998/12/redmond/.

World Scholarship Forum. "Ongoing Blacks at Microsoft Scholarship 2021–2022." April 12, 2021. https://worldscholarshipforum.com/blacks-at-microsoft-scholarships-2017/.

Index